# RLS
## IN LOVE

# RLS
## IN LOVE

*The Love Poetry of*
ROBERT LOUIS STEVENSON

# Stuart Campbell

**SANDSTONEPRESS**
HIGHLAND | SCOTLAND

First published in Great Britain by
Sandstone Press Ltd
PO Box 5725
One High Street
Dingwall
Ross-shire
IV15 9WJ
Scotland.

*www.sandstonepress.com*

The publisher acknowledges subsidy from the Scottish Arts Council
towards publication of this volume.

ISBN-10: 1-905207-28-X
ISBN-13: 978-1-905207-28-2

Jacket design by Gravemaker + Scott, Edinburgh

Typeset in Monotype Perpetua by Iolaire Typesetting, Newtonmore.
Printed and bound by Bell & Bain, Glasgow

**Mixed Sources**
Product group from well-managed
forests and other controlled sources
www.fsc.org  Cert no. TT-COC-002769
© 1996 Forest Stewardship Council

FSC

# CONTENTS

## THE POEMS

### Part One
## The Swinging Gait of Harlots
### 49

### Part Two
## A Long Despair
### 69

### Part Three
## The One Illogical Adventure
### 91

# ACKNOWLEDGEMENTS

I am grateful to a large number of people who have provided me with endless help, advice and encouragement. They include; Jenny Renton, Claire Harman, Robyn Marsack, Elaine Greig, Denise Brace, Ken Paterson, Colin MacConnachie, Kerry Houston, Alan Rennie, Catriona McPherson, my father-in-law, Robert Mclaughlan, Rona McBrierty, Tom, Amy, Alice and Morag, my own Tiger Lily.

I would also like to thank Robert Davidson, Moira Forsyth and Iain Gordon of Sandstone Press for having faith in me and nurturing me through the whole process.

I also acknowledge the Beinecke Rare Book and Manuscript Library Yale University, The Writers Museum Edinburgh, City of Edinburgh Library Services and the Stevenson estate.

And a final nod to Cheltenham Town Football Club whose perennial struggles with relegation have meant many long journeys with lap top.

ACKNOWLEDGEMENTS

# LIST OF PHOTOGRAPHIC PLATES

1 Alison Cunningham Stevenson's nurse
(Reproduced courtesy of the Writers Museum, Edinburgh)

2 Swanston Village 2008
(Reproduced courtesy of Robert Mclaughlan)

3 The Bridge at Grez 2008
(Taken by the author)

4 Rutherfords Bar Edinburgh 2009
(Reproduced courtesy of Ken Paterson)

5 Fanny Sitwell
(Lucas, E.V., *The Colvins and Their Friends* (London)), 1928)

6 Katherine de Mattos
(City of Edinburgh Art Collection)

7 RLS 1880 aged 29 in the year of his marriage
(Reproduced courtesy of the Writers Museum, Edinburgh)

8 Fanny Osbourne 1880
(Reproduced courtesy of the Writers Museum, Edinburgh)

9 Hillside Sketch
(From the author's collection)

*The Love Poetry of*
# ROBERT LOUIS STEVENSON

## STUART CAMPBELL

Bright is the ring of words
    When the right man rings them,
Fair the fall of songs
    When the singer sings them.
Still they carolled and said –
    On wings they are carried –
After the singer is dead
    And the maker buried.

Low as the singer lies
    In the field of heather,
Songs of his fashion bring
    The swains together.
And when the west is read
    With the sunset embers,
The lover lingers and sings
    And the maid remembers.
                 *(Songs of Travel)*

'I wish I had made more of a religion of sex.' This is not DH Lawrence, who was only eight years old at the time, but Robert Louis Stevenson in a letter to his cousin Bob.

Middle-class Edinburgh, always wanting to claim RLS as its own, has consistently selected those aspects of his behaviour that most closely corresponded to Victorian and indeed early twenty first century New Town respectability. Pride in his attendance at the Edinburgh Academy, for example, Stevenson hated the place. His later courtship of tavern women was much more than a self-indulgent attempt to recreate himself as a free spirit and a bit of a lad, although there was sufficient of the Calvin in RLS for him to feel ambivalent about his own conduct.

In the years after his death the Establishment drew a discrete veil over this aspect of his life: whoring and adultery were mere peccadilloes, of no more significance than the prank that led to Stevenson, the naughty snowballing student, being bound over for breach of the peace in the shadow of Surgeon's Hall. There was a collective, condescending attempt to protect the prodigy from himself by censoring references to those episodes that would do his reputation no good whatsoever.

A backlash against the misplaced critical collusion was inevitable. Sooner or later lids would blow. Suppression gave way to a whole cottage industry in speculation about the identity of the various women that Stevenson had allegedly lusted after, yearned for and bedded. There is, however, no smoke without a cliché and much of the speculation, although probably wrong, has a sort of truth that will be unashamedly rehashed on these pages. There may be an element of prurience in the speculation but the bottom line is that Stevenson's love life and his attitude to sex is a hugely important area in our understanding of his work.

In his early days there is evidence that Stevenson thoroughly enjoyed a stint as pornographer. Eve Blantyre describes how Stevenson, James Ferrier and Walter, her brother, made up a trio of inveterate boozers who spent a lot of time and money in the Gay Japanee, the Green

Elephant, The Twinkling Eye and other such dubious Edinburgh drinking dens. They set themselves a competition to write the most depraved novella imaginable, something that would personify the 'terribleness, outrageous blackness of human depravity' Needless to say, Stevenson won with a truly appalling tale called *The History of Peru*, presumably the *Fanny Hill* of its time. What price the manuscript now?

Stevenson consistently cultivated and manipulated his image: to an extent he collaborated with the fictionalising of his own character. That he was successful in this endeavour is reflected in the continuing confusion between the man and his work. The bewildering range of genres, mastered or merely tinkered with, provide a whole circus tent of reflecting mirrors.

Robert Louis Stevenson was a prolific poet, as the weight and size of Roger C Lewis's definitive anthology makes abundantly clear. He wrote elegies, ballads, verse letters, poems in English, Scots and French. He wrote roundels, sonnets and odes. He stole from the metaphysical poets, aped the Romantics and drooled for a while over Whitman. He wrote poetry about politics, history, religion, travel, friends and family. The experience of looking at the thick corpus of his poetry is like that of a child staring at a puzzle of dots and lines trying to see the hidden shape which, once seen, cannot be unseen: Robert Louis Stevenson, love poet.

Stevenson's love poetry, anthologized for the first time here, provides insight into this crucial aspect of his life. A chronological scrutiny of these poems enables us to chart fresh territory: not only the significant milestones in his personal journey but also patterns of emotional development from his turbulent student days to the deceptively serene years in Samoa.

Anyone compiling an anthology of Stevenson's poetry must acknowledge the debt to one of his earliest biographers, George Hellman. Often seen as an eccentric obsessive rather than a serious scholar

Hellman occupies a strange place among Stevenson's critics. His role as wheeler-dealer in the New York auction rooms in the 1920s, when Belle finally agreed to part with her step father's unpublished manuscripts, did little to enhance his standing as an editor working on behalf of the Boston Bibliophile Society. He perpetrated the unforgivable crime of arbitrarily bundling up and binding the papers, before selling them to private collectors. At a stroke he made all but impossible the task of dating or contextualising many of Stevenson's previously unpublished poems.

Most of the main players in Stevenson's life were still alive when Hellman published *The True Stevenson A Study in Clarification* in 1925 which has been criticized for its many cavalier claims and apparent innacuracies. It was though, less important to produce endless footnotes and learned references when you were on talking terms with people who had known Stevenson intimately. This non-scholarly tendency persisted throughout the 20th century. Many reputable biographers have chosen to repeat rumours and gossip, about Edinburgh's favourite, if errant son.

In Hellman's time the rumours were red hot. Many were concerned with the belief that Stevenson's widow had on at least two occasions destroyed manuscripts, fearful for what the sexually explicit content would do for her husband's carefully nurtured reputation. It was alleged that Fanny, incensed that the author of *A Child's Garden of Verses* would even think of publishing a novel whose central character was a street-walker, thrust the manuscript into the fire. This would of course have been the second manuscript to receive this particular treatment if we accept that she had also forced Stevenson to consign an early version of *Dr. Jekyll and Mr Hyde* to the flames on account of the explicitly sexual nature of Hyde's vice.

Hellman took particular issue with Sidney Colvin, Stevenson's lifelong friend, sometime rival in love and failed biographer. Their correspondence in the New York Tribune was acrimonious particularly when Colvin argued strongly that Hellman should never have published the poems in the first place.

Hellman justified his decision; 'Many of these poems have, of course, to do with Stevenson's early affairs of the heart, and include a long series of poems addressed to a young woman who he deeply and finely loved. Indeed, this love episode, known to Mrs Fleeming Jenkins, and others of Stevenson's friends, reflects, it seems to me, credit and not discredit on the generous and chivalrous Stevenson. But you seem to consider all the evidences of these early romances as matters that the reader has no right to know, nor ''should have the desire, apart from mere prurience, to know''. It would be amusing to consider a life of Byron, or of Shelley, written from such a point of view . . .' Indeed.

Colvin defended his own position by declaring that Stevenson had a total hatred of 'Public prying into private lives, the promulgation by the press, and printing of private letters during a writer's lifetime.' By way of justification he then conjures a bizarre picture of Stevenson, who 'gave himself a dangerous cold by dancing before a bonfire in the garden at the news of a society editor who had been committed to prison.'

Hellman rightly recognizes that Colvin was hardly a disinterested figure in this debate as many of the poems that he objected to were inspired by the woman whom he would eventually marry. This particularly tangled web provides the context for the poetry in the second part of the anthology.

JA Steuart nailed his colours to the mast in his choice of quotation to preface his 1924 biography *RLS Man and Writer* 'If you are so seriously pained by the misconduct of your subject and so paternally delighted with his virtues, you will always be an excellent gentleman, but a somewhat questionable biographer.'

To an extent Stevenson did collude in the suppression of his early love poems. Much has been made of the fact that he chose not to publish them during his lifetime. There can only be two reasons for this. Perhaps he was so appalled or embarrassed by the quality of his early verse that he didn't want them to see the light of day, condemning them instead to rot away in the ever growing archive devoted to unfinished, unloved or merely abandoned pieces. The other possibility is that he didn't wish to cause offence to anyone, or upset his 'Tiger Lily'. With the possible exception of Fanny Sitwell, Colvin's future wife, it is difficult to see who could possibly be embarrassed by the publication of the early poems. Only one of them specifically included a recognisable name, Jennie or Jeannie; one other has the name Claire in the margin, of which more anon, and one other provides the reference to the quarryman's daughter that has fuelled speculation about Stevenson's fevered trysting in the Swanston dells.

The annotations in the margins of many of the poems *pas mal*, etc, show that he did in fact revisit them at a later time. It is difficult to tell if his comments are genuinely dismissive or ironically self-deprecatory. In any case, who knows how many poems were crumpled and tossed into the sea from the deck of the Casco or any of the other schooners that eventually carried the Stevensons across the oceans.

Many of the poems that were not intended for publication during his lifetime are cameos of raw, unpolished emotion containing a strong therapeutic element, as if, through attempting verse, Stevenson strove to make his overwhelming depression manageable. Often he failed. Many of the poems are unfinished and abandoned and while this makes them poor from a critical perspective, they have a real psychological power that justifies their inclusion in this anthology.

The link between bi polar disorder and creativity is well established and it has become fashionable to recruit a whole legion of dead writers and composers under the banner of manic depression. The label is only useful in so far as it helps capture the profound shift in mood states that characterises the condition. It also provides a context for writers who have been dismissed as dilettantes, whose work is characterised by unevenness, inconsistency and a tendency to embark on myriad unfinished projects. All of these accusations have been levelled at Stevenson. There is also evidence that creativity does not just coincide with the hypermanic aspect of the condition but can also be a product of the depressed phase. Several of the poems in this anthology were written when Stevenson was in the grip of near suicidal despair. The important aspect is that many of them have survived, albeit in a form that does not invite critical acclaim. The label bi polar has other implications for the way Stevenson wrote. For writers whose creative rhythm is dictated in part by their position on the bi polar scale at any one time, revision and reworking during periods of 'normality' become crucial. This in turn would explain why so many of Stevenson's love poems have been through multiple drafts to the extent that it is often difficult to identify their subject. These perspectives are explored further in the notes in the section that follows the poems.

Today Stevenson's illness would be labelled rapid cycle bi polar disorder. He could travel the road from exhilaration to total despair in the course of a single day. JA Steuart noted 'if his mercurial temperament leaped up in the sun, it plunged as quickly to zero in the shade.'

In March 1870 Stevenson writes to his cousin Bob; 'My dear Bob, During almost the whole of this winter, I have been free from my usual attacks of morbid mealancholy . . . but today I was in the depths again . . . Yesterday I was in high spirits . . . But from the morning I was gone, tried to find out where I could get Haschish, half-determined to get drunk and ended (as usual) by going to a graveyard. I stayed about two hours in Greyfriars Churchyard in the depths of wretchedness.' Stevenson dabbled with drugs at various stages in his life, the idea of self medication to offset the effects of mental ill health is not a new concept.

The facts are few. In his early days Stevenson enjoyed the company of prostitutes; he later became besotted with Fanny Sitwell; he eventually married Fanny Osbourne, for better or for worse, and succumbed emotionally and, perhaps, sexually to a succession of women throughout his life.

The poems though, show a more complex emotional chronology than is suggested by these ostensibly discrete phases. Rarely does Stevenson capture and celebrate the spontaneous joy of the moment. Present time is viewed from an imagined future, while ghosts from his past constantly jostle shoulders with current obsessions. He even wrote poems to women he had not yet met.

A consistently challenging strand of his love poetry was Stevenson's tendency to idealise every woman he encountered. A common trait perhaps, but one that has directly fuelled the speculation about the detail of his love life and the identity of his lovers. The later poems to Fanny Sitwell demonstrate conclusively that when his sexual advances were rebuffed, or were inappropriate, he resorted to sublimation by idealising the object of his anguish.

This process of idealisation served as a convenient mask hiding the whores and harlots whose flesh he enjoyed, his cousins for whom his affections were probably entirely honourable, and his friends' sisters for whom his feelings were in all likelihood not untainted with lust.

# 1 THE SWINGING GAIT OF HARLOTS

Most, but far from all, of the speculation about Stevenson's love life is concerned with the years between 1870 and 1875.

Before this period, the counterpane years of childhood were characterised by ill health, frequent nightmares induced by the hellfire inspired bedtime stories told by Cummy, his nurse, and moments of innocent rapture at both Colinton and Heriot Row.

The annual family holidays at North Berwick provide the first source of romantic speculation, an early dalliance over the rock pools with Katherine de Mattos, his younger cousin who joined them at the holiday home. His fondness for her remained undiminished by time and is expressed with an ambiguous intensity in several of his later poems.

The speculation only starts with Katherine de Mattos. Whose hand did he furtively brush in the pew? Whose hand did he hold when skating on Duddingston Loch? Which young woman from the New Town bourgeoisie did he fall for when taking part in the amateur dramatics at the Jenkins' house? Which servant did he press himself against on the stairs?

Swanston provided ample opportunity for emotional entanglement. The precise identity of the women Stevenson lay with in the shadow of the Pentlands is irrelevant. It doesn't matter if she was the daughter of the quarryman or of the blacksmith, although the romantic connotations of the latter occupation might have had more appeal for him.

What could be of more consequence in retrospect is the social standing of his rustic amours. It is difficult to think of a single occasion when Stevenson was attracted to someone of whom his father was likely to have approved. There was something almost perverse about his choices. Perhaps we should not be surprised that Stevenson senior was wonderfully phlegmatic when his son merely chose to pursue an American divorcee, given his dubious track record with the local lasses and the prostitutes whom he had threatened to bring home to Heriot Row.

Swanston was the perfect backcloth for the magic lantern show of his idealised loves. When he paints the village in the intense hues of hindsight, it emerges as an impossible arcadia, somewhere between Brigadoon and a courtly love tapestry. Having said that, the gentrified Swanston of today is still stunningly beautiful, as is for that matter the river that flows through Grez (plates 2&3). If Stevenson chose for his love affairs those milieus whose lilies needed no further gilding, then perhaps too we should not assume that the portraits of his mistresses and lovers are unrealistically idealised.

A feature of Swanston that may have a symbolic bearing on Stevenson's love life is its location. By walking fifty yards out of the village towards Allermuir the whole panorama of Edinburgh is revealed like a distant country. If he looked to the left of the castle he would have seen the old and new towns, the twin spheres of his different lives. He could have traced his route from brothel and tavern to hearth and home.

Ian Bell in *Dreams of Exile* suggests that the fact that Stevenson was never late for his tea at Heriot Row gives the lie to the idea that he spent many waking hours revelling in the company of High Street whores. I'm not so sure. Stevenson wasn't an admirer of Deacon Brodie for nothing. He clearly had a sneaky respect for the embodiment of bourgeois respectability who combined cabinet making with house-breaking. Compared with this exquisite piece of multi-tasking, fitting amorous encounters round the family meal would not have been difficult.

One name above all others is associated with these encounters; Claire. Biographers and scandal mongers alike have seized on the name written in the margins of a single poem and speculated that Claire, whoever she was, must have been the love of Stevenson's life. Was she a working girl in the pub-cum-brothel at the foot of Carlton Hill or a willing nymph to Stevenson's shepherd in the shadow of the Pentlands? According to JC Furnas in *Voyage to Windward,* Claire didn't exist. The name was one of many that the lovelorn Louis bestowed on Fanny Sitwell. Although this was certainly the case, as is amply confirmed by the letters, JA Stewart may not have been far off the mark when he confidently declared that Claire was simply a *nom de guerre*, (or more accurately a *nom d'amour*): Claire was code for his current obsession. This theory would exonerate Katherine Osbourne from the accusation of malicious lunacy when she wrote to Hellman 'I have been told just now – as though it was a secret – by one of S's relatives about Louis' first and great love. The girl's name was Claire, or Clara. Mary and Maggie or Maggie (sic) must have been the Edinburgh girl or girls. S himself never made any secret of his love affairs only as far as he shielded the woman . . . Claire was a blacksmith's daughter . . .'

JA Steuart further suggested that one of Claire's manifestations was Kate Drummond, 'described to me by one who saw her as slim and dark, very trim and neat, with jet black hair and a complexion that needed no cosmetics to make it rosy and alluring'. This last detail certainly rings true judging by Stevenson's declared hankering for the touch of a dusky woman.

So obsessive did JA Steuart become with his theory, he wrote *The Cap of Honour*, a full-length 'autobiographical' novel purporting to be based on a lost Stevenson manuscript.

Frank McGlyn in *Robert Louis Stevenson: A Biography* set the Claire among the hounds again by suggesting that the name was probably a working title for a novel that Stevenson planned to write but never did.

Fact or figment, whore or nymph, if Claire remains an enigma, there is no such mystery surrounding Mary H. She was real. Stevenson once declared his love 'of the publican and harlot', and Mary unashamedly belonged to the latter category. Even Balfour acknowledged her existence in a letter to Colvin in which he pompously and euphemistically refers to 'the seasons of temptation. Most strongly besetting the ardent and poetic temperament, to seek solace among the crude allurements of the city streets.' There is speculation that she was the prostitute that Louis told his parents that he intended to bring home to Heriot Row as his wife. The extent of the parental apoplexy can only be guessed at. It would have made for a more interesting piece of drama than his turgid collaborative efforts with WE Henley.

Clare Harman quotes at length in *Robert Louis Stevenson A Biography* from Stevenson's unpublished and unfinished autobiography in which he describes a subsequent meeting with Mary H.

'She was a robust, great-haunched, blue-eyed young woman of admirable temper and, if you will let me say so of a prostitute, extraordinary modesty. Every now and again she would go to work; once, I remember, for some months in a factory down Leith Walk, from which I often met her returning; but when she was not upon the streets, she did not choose to be recognised. She was perfectly self-respecting. I had certainly small fatuity at that period; for it never occurred to me that she thought of me accept in the way of business, though now remember her attempts to waken my jealousy which, being very simple, I took at the time for gospel. Years and years after all this was over and gone, when I was walking sick and sorry and alone, I met Mary somewhat carefully dressed; and we recognised each other with a joy that was, I daresay, a surprise to both. I spent three or four hours with her in a public-house parlour; she was going to emigrate in a few days to America; we had much to talk about; and she cried bitterly, and so did I. We found in that interview that we had been dear friends without knowing it; I can still hear her recalling the past in her sober, Scotch voice, and I can still feel her good honest loving hand as we said goodbye.'

No wonder that emotional ghosts feature in his love poems. The phrase 'we had been friends without knowing it' also resonates ironically with the poems written to Fanny Sitwell, in which his determination to be her friend hides much more. Stevenson also questions the assumptions he made about the purely business nature of his relationship with Mary H. Many of the poems show the same wish to reclaim and perhaps redefine the past.

Then, as now, engaging with prostitutes carried health risks. There are sufficient references in the letters to justify the conclusion that Stevenson did suffer periodically from a sexually transmitted disease, probably syphilis. Mary H may be one of 'the unblushing daughters of Venus who did him a lasting injury'. If Stevenson did contract syphilis from a prostitute, what impact did that have on subsequent relationships? Could it have been a trigger for the profound depression that was also a frequent and unwanted visitor during these formative years? The pox was no laughing matter, and certainly not for someone as emotionally and sexually charged as Stevenson, even if he did maintain that it was 'better to loose health as a spendthrift than to waste it as a miser.'

There was something odd about Stevenson's attitude to prostitutes. That he revelled in their company was a source of pride, a perverse badge of social distinction: 'I was the companion of seamen, chimney sweeps, and thieves . . . At this time I used to have my headquarters in an old public house frequented by the lowest order of prostitutes.' This may have been Rutherfords Bar (plate 4). He would boast of his prowess claiming that very few could resist him. 'I have been all my days a dead hand at a harridan.' Perhaps his boast, thrown off like a Wildean aphorism, shows more concern for shock value than veracity. As Frank McGlyn notes, he conveniently ignores the possibility that their interest was grounded more in financial considerations than mutual attraction.

There is no denying that Stevenson felt great empathy with the lives of prostitutes, as Lloyd Osbourne, his step-son, testified. Tom Stevenson also, in the grand tradition of Victorian philanthropy, and possibly hypocrisy too, acknowledged the harshness of their plight. This innuendo is not original, it was first voiced by the redoubtable Katherine Osbourne who in her lengthy correspondence with Hellman comments, 'I had always thought that Louis' father had something on his own conscience that he was always doing for fallen women, and was the more severe with his son.'

Stevenson's letters reveal ambivalence to this period in his life. In an early letter to his cousin Bob, who he refers to as his safety valve, he adopts a Calvinist tone that would have greatly pleased Cummy ' . . . relationship is but the body, friendship the soul; without the latter, the former is a corpse too heavy for the pair to drag between them and often corrupting in their very hands'. There may be a clue here which casts light on the tendency to idealise. The gratification of lust is only acceptable within the context of friendship, hence the need to engage at a deeper level with the street women with whom he associated.

In a later letter to Trevor Haddon, an admiring art student with whom he frequently corresponded, Stevenson argues the exact opposite, and warns against elevating lust into something ostensibly nobler:

'. . . if you can keep your sexual desires in order, be glad, be very glad. Some day when you meet your fate, you will be free, and the better man. Don't make a boy or girl friendship into something it is not. The brothel is a more ennobling spot (in our society, which is not ideal) than any amourette... Whatever you do, see that you don't sacrifice a woman . . . Avoid the primness of your virtue; hardness to a poor harlot is a far lower sin than the ugliest unchastity.'

This theme is developed further in the letter which provided the initial quote for this essay. The full text from Stevenson's last letter to Bob is as follows:

'If I had to begin again – I know not – *si jeunesse savait, si vieillesse pouvait.* – I know not at all – I believe I should do as I have done– except I believe that I should try to be more chaste in early youth, and honour Sex more religiously. The damned thing of our education is that Christianity does not recognise and hallow sex. It looks askance at it, over its shoulder, oppressed as it is by reminiscences of hermits and Asiatic self torturers. When I came to myself fairly about twenty- five I recognised once for all the Lingam and the Yoni as the true religious symbols. An eye might also do. It is a terrible hiatus in our modern religions that they cannot see and make venerable that which they ought to see first and hallow most. Well, it is so: I cannot be wiser than my generation.'

Stevenson was wiser than most of his generation, although judging by the frequent expressions of self-worthlessness that characterised many of his earlier letters to cousin Bob, he too engaged in mental torment that would not have disgraced the efforts of the aforementioned Asiatic self torturers.

JA Steuart was among the first of Stevenson's biographers to identify an attitude towards sex that is at best pompous and confused and at worst, hypocritical. He quotes from the early smug and censorious essay on Burns which he sums up as 'a dishonest performance unworthy alike of its subject and its author . . . there is something comically ironical in the spectacle of the Stevenson of that period delivering sermons on the amatory irregularities of Robert Burns.'

Leaving aside for the time being both the philosophical and sexual health aspects of Stevenson's relationship with prostitutes, he was also leaving himself open to blackmail. One interpretation placed on a letter to WE Henley is that a street woman had threatened to blow the gaff at the very moment when his passion for Fanny Osbourne was at its most intense. This in turn led him to come clean with his father about his intentions towards the nomadic American artist he had befriended in the woods of Fontainebleau.

This belongs in the future. When not playing his own version of nymphs and shepherds or seeking solace at the hands of the women whose descendents still eke out an exploited living in Edinburgh's numerous saunas and massage parlours, Velvet Coat, as he was known on account of his bohemian appearance, was happily cultivating a taste for the older woman. Ian Bell may not have been far wrong when he snorted that this was perhaps the destination of a whole generation of cosseted youth reared by their nannies.

For Stevenson the first known recipient of his displaced nanny syndrome was Anne Jenkin, part of the formidable husband and wife team into whose company and favour he insinuated himself. A ready made, alternative family just down the road in The New Town Edinburgh, who represented everything his own parents were not: fun, theatrical, eccentric and welcoming. Professor Jenkin had had the earlier misfortune of tutoring his young neighbour who was playing at studying for a degree in engineering. The disaffected student then proceeded to become infatuated with the professor's beautiful and gifted wife. If it wasn't for the evidence that Stevenson revered the professor and treated him as a surrogate father, this could be construed as revenge, or indeed as the plot for one of the many plays enacted by the family and friends before invited audiences. No wonder the frustrated youth fell in love with the woman who was variously Cleopatra, Katherine the shrew, Griselda and Mrs. Malaprop.

WE Henley, Stevenson's close friend, astute critic and the unwitting model for Long John Silver, was fully aware of his prodegy's love of the stage. In his hagiographic poem, *Apparition*, Henley observed that Stevenson's own theatricality would have suited him equally to the roles of Puck, Ariel and Hamlet. Between them the ill matched pair could have acted out the entire canon. Jenkin however kept the doting and smitten Stevenson firmly in his place, or at least kept him in the wings allowing him no more than the occasional walk on part. To exhaust the metaphor, this transient infatuation was no more than a dress rehearsal for the real thing.

# 2 A LONG DESPAIR

If the Cornhill Magazine had run a lonely hearts column in the latter part of the nineteenth century the following might have appeared: 'Spindly young man, WLTM older woman, with a view to friendship, possibly more.'

Oedipus is often pushed centre stage to explain why Stevenson was attracted to a certain type of woman. His mother and the nightmare inducing Cummy (plate 1) are seen as key influences in his romantic choices. The exclusive nature of his parents' marriage is cited as prompting orphan like behaviour in our hero, and the associated craving for the approval of older women.

Be that as it may, his involvement with the Jenkin family and his attraction for Mrs. J under the benevolent but complicit eye of the Professor, established a formula that was to repeat itself at Cockfield Rectory in the idyllic surroundings of the Suffolk countryside.

Embarking on an emotional sabbatical from the stifling parental brew of disapproval and inappropriate expectations, Stevenson readily agreed to take time out in the home of Maud Babbington, his mother's cousin. It is difficult to underestimate the impact that Stevenson had on his hosts, and their long term guest, Fanny Sitwell (plate 5).

Whereas as Stevenson subsequently declared in his essay *On falling in love*, 'A wet rag goes safely by the fire'; in fact his dry wit and manic erudition made an immediate conflagration inevitable. He was instantly consumed by passion for the 34 year old Fanny Sitwell whom

Claire Harman describes as 'Sibylline, sensitive, brave, tender, bereaved, abused' adding 'he would have fallen in love with a tenth of her'. Fanny was separated from her clergyman husband, a man of 'uncongenial habits' according to EV Lucas in *The Colvins and their Friends*. Presumably these habits extended beyond picking his toenails. Stevenson would never refer to him by name, preferring instead the less than flattering epithet 'incubus' or merely identifying him as 'letter 22 of the alphabet'. Presumably V stood for vicar, but vile, villain and voluptuary are also contenders.

Fanny had initially followed her errant husband to a parish in Calcutta before returning to London's East End to avoid the cholera outbreak. When she met Stevenson she was employed as secretary and translator to the College for Men and Women, an institution that defied convention by teaching both sexes in the same classroom.

A potentially more formidable obstacle to the romance than her husband was the cadaverous figure of Sidney Colvin, but here things become less clear. Fanny was the recipient of emotional support and intellectual stimulation from Colvin who at the time was Slade Professor of Fine Art at Cambridge. The ostensibly shy and socially awkward Colvin would use Fanny as a convenient female companion and hostess when he wished to impress visiting members of his artistic coterie. After meeting her astonishing young guest from Edinburgh, Fanny waxed lyrical about his merits to Colvin who proceeded post-haste to Cockfield to meet their latest prodigy, and was instantly impressed. In a lengthy passage from his *Memories and Notes* Colvin provides one of the most affectionate portraits ever penned of the man who inspired not a few paeans of praise during his lifetime and eulogies after his death:

'If you want to realise the kind of effect he made, at least in the early years when I knew him best, imagine this attenuated but extraordinarily vivid and vital presence, with something about it that first struck you as freakish, rare, fantastic, a touch of the elfin and unearthly, a sprite, an Ariel. And imagine that, as you got to know him, this sprite, this visitant from another sphere, turned out to differ from mankind in general not by being less human but by being a great deal more human than they; richer-blooded, greater-hearted; more human in all senses of the word, for he comprised within himself, and would flash on you in the course of a single afternoon, all the different ages and half the different characters of man, the unfaded freshness of a child, the ardent outlook and adventurous day-dreams of a boy, the steadfast courage of manhood, the quick sympathetic tenderness of a woman, and already, as early as the mid twenties of his life, an almost uncanny share of the ripe life-wisdom of old age. He was a fellow of infinite and unrestrained jest and yet of infinite earnest, the one very often a mask for the other; a poet, an artist, an adventurer; a man beset with fleshly frailties, and despite his infirm health of strong appetites and unchecked curiosities; and yet a profoundly sincere moralist and preacher and son of the Covenanters . . .'

Colvin had occasion to observe at first hand the fleshly frailties and strong appetites as Stevenson laid siege to Fanny Sitwell.

There is something elusive and odd about the *ménage a trois* or *quatre*, if the appalling vicar is included. Despite the fact that Fanny wallowed in the attention of her ardent swain and was devoted to him, there is no evidence that the sexual attraction was reciprocal. There are various ambiguous references in Stevenson's letters, and a fragment of a poem, hinting at significant events but it is impossible to place these events on an erotic spectrum that stretches from kissing chastely in the conservatory to consummation in the Suffolk fields. Speculation is inevitable, if for no other reason than the fact that Fanny asked that her side of the correspondence be destroyed. Her charitable but bland recollections published half a century later in Rosaline Masson's *I Remember Robert Louis Stevenson* do nothing to fill the void.

Equally elusive is Colvin's real attitude to the blossoming relationship between the woman he would himself marry twenty five years later and the love-lorn Stevenson.

In *Voyage to Windward* JC Furnas resorts to mangled syntax in his attempt to explain the strained platonic dance that took place at Cockfield. 'Utter belief in technical chastity as a moral and aesthetic value could greatly have minimised the ill effects of thwarting biological urges.' Of the three Stevenson was the least adept at thwarting his biological impulses.

Many years later after tending to his dying mother with whom he lived Colvin, at the age of sixty four, married Fanny Sitwell. The vicar had been dead for six years and Stevenson for eleven. For a quarter of a century Colvin kept his council, and his powder dry while Fanny continued courting a small galaxy of bright young literary stars. He would eventually write of her;

'In the fearlessness of her purity she can afford the frankness of her affections, and shows how every fascination of her sex may in the most open freedom be the most honourably secure. Yet in a world of men and women, such an one cannot walk without kindling once and again a dangerous flame before she is aware. As in her nature there is no room for vanity, she never foresees these masculine combustions, but has a wonderful art and gentleness in allaying them, and is accustomed to convert the claims and cravings of passion into the lifelong loyalty of grateful and contented friendship.'

It is possible that Colvin himself revealed a more intense emotional and sexual ardour towards Stevenson than Fanny. In his hyperbolic words of praise, Stevenson is an amalgam of child, boy, man and woman. Jenni Calder in *Robert Louis Stevenson: A Life Study* was the first to hint at Colvin's own sexuality as a factor in the equation. Like Prospero with a speech impediment, Colvin skilfully stage manages the passion that his mentor vainly lavishes on Fanny. Stevenson himself

*21*

declared that Colvin 'burns with a mild, steady flame of exaggeration towards all whom he likes and regards'.

Colvin would later emerge as the self appointed guardian of Stevenson's reputation. There was to be no slight on either his personal morality or sexual behaviour. As his controversial editorship of the letters demonstrated, he tried to shape Stevenson's posthumous reputation to suit his own ends. Colvin was always playing a long game, one in which he enjoyed significant success. Stevenson's affection towards the older man far outlasted his desperate longing for Fanny Sitwell. Indeed his feelings for Colvin remained constant throughout his subsequent marriage to the second Fanny in his life. After initially flattering Stevenson's wife, Colvin later tried with WE Henley to bury her with faint praise.

When Colvin married Fanny in 1901 the game was squared. Or not quite. He still had a soul to claim. In the 1920s Colvin published the essay *Fleeming and Anne Jenkin* choosing to retread the same ground that Stevenson had previously covered in his own tribute to the deceased Professor, but also using the opportunity to throw his suffocating cloak of praise over Anne Jenkin. He was effectively laying posthumous claim to yet another woman who at one time ruled Stevenson's heart.

We know little about the detail of the first five weeks Stevenson spent at Cockfield. We have small idyllic glimpses; Colvin walloping a cricket ball into the midriff of an unsuspecting small boy, one of the 110 school children for whom Stevenson was making sandwiches. He subsequently used his blistered knife holding hand as an excuse for not writing as much as was normal. His persona is closer to Peter Pan and the Pied Piper than to Lothario.

He wrote only five letters that we know of during this time, four to his mother and one to Charles Baxter. To his mother he declared he was 'too happy to be much of a correspondent'. He wisely kept quiet about the reason for his growing rapture, preferring instead to tell her what she probably wanted to hear; that Scotland was better than England on every count and that he was finding time to glance at his law books. No references in the letters to the idyllic hours spent wandering through the countryside with an older married woman on his arm, no poems, either, celebrating the ecstasy of resting his head in Fanny Sitwell's lap.

After the blissful sojourn in Suffolk the return to Edinburgh and a flood of letters. The need to convey in letters his every thought, memory and hope directly to his beloved meant that there was little time for poetry. He wrote, 'I have tried to write some verses; but I find I have nothing to say that has not been already perfectly said.'

The letters themselves become ever more finely crafted until Stevenson hits on the expedient of basing a novel, provisionally entitled *Claire* on the exchange of letters between them. The project however was still-born from the moment she made it clear that her letters were to be destroyed, and that his were never to be published in her lifetime.

When reading Booth and Mehew's *The Letters of Robert Louis Stevenson*, the one sided nature of the correspondence is tantalising. 'We have both (as you say) a main unpleasant road to travel and we must hold hands firmly and mutually keep up our hearts.'

What words had Fanny used to elicit this response? And when he wrote pompously, 'I have swung my censor before no empty shrine.' Did her reply encourage him to persevere with the religious analogy, which is destined to become ever more strained, or does she tell him not to be so stupid and keep his sexual metaphors to himself?

Life on the home front reached its nadir in a furious barney with his dad, a man not without mental health issues himself. Thomas Stevenson, snatching at ever more bizarre theories to explain away everything that was bad, bohemian or downright bewildering about his son, basically decided that a big boy had done it and run away: Cousin

Bob was the scapegoat, the diabolic influence. He was banished from the Stevenson household. We can picture Bob punching the air out of sheer relief, and Stevenson rushing upstairs, pen in hand, to give Fanny a blow by blow account of his latest misery.

Ever more anguished by his feelings for Fanny, Stevenson told his mother he was popping down to Carlisle for some reason and simply kept going until he arrived in London and was reunited with her and Colvin. They took one look at him, and marched him off to the obliging Dr Clark who promptly prescribed a holiday in the South of France.

After the initial euphoria of arriving in a foreign place, and firmly believing that his old kitbag contained none of his troubles, his spirits plummeted again. His mind was 'a constant quiet simmer of you' as he wrote to Fanny. The simmering boiled over and he sought refuge in opium. Stevenson had graduated from hashish in the graveyard to mind expanding drugs in a hotel room.

After one such indulgence he looks back on a day of extraordinary happiness and a night that was characterised by 'something almost terrifying in the pleasures that besieged me in the darkness. Wonderful tremors filled me; my head swam in the most delirious manner, and the bed softly oscillated with me, like a boat in a very gentle ripple.' Judging by its cosmic scale the poem *Swallows travel to and fro* was conceived in the same hallucinogenic fog.

Under the influence of opium he wrote to Mrs Sitwell on December 7th 1873 a letter of astoundingly sentimental drivel about a violet that reduced him to tears of wonder. The letter is enough to reduce anyone to tears.

Apart from the pharmaceutical indulgence of opium, there were other distractions. The fact that the hotel at Mentone seemed to incorporate the entire cast from a Restoration comedy was to his taste. The main players were Mme Zassatsky and her entourage. Initially flattered by the attentions of yet another older woman, Stevenson seemed more than willing to embrace the possibilities presented by his eclectic companions. Or almost. It seems likely that Mme Z would have been more than happy to join Stevenson in the odd embrace, and probably much, much more. But she caught our convalescent off balance.

The attentions of this aristocratic siren seem to have frightened Stevenson witless. She was an arch fantasist, variously described as a princess and a religious fanatic. By her own account she had a reputation as a midwife in league with the devil. She formed a formidable double act with her younger sister. JC Furnas in *Voyage to Windward* splutters, 'The elder Mme Zassatsky, was an ironic, impulsive, hag ridden backhanded kind of Slavic liberal, mother of ten and alleged author of successful comedies.' Perhaps she cast Stevenson in the role of stuttering innocent, a vulnerable but valuable foil to her self-conscious theatrical machinations. Furnas comments that Stevenson had little answer to the sisters' 'emotional nudity'.

From his first encounter with the Russians he was perplexed and admitted he understood them 'not at all; not in the least'. He was soon caught up in a world where nothing was quite what it seemed. The sisters confused him completely over which one of them was in fact the mother to Bella, the small child in their company. Not content with flirting over the samovar, Mme Z caused him all manner of angst by fondling his hand under pretence of examining it for some unspecified reason. He describes the incident in a letter to Fanny Sitwell, apparently incurring her jealousy, judging by his response to the curt letter he received by return. He also sent her poems celebrating the wicked sisters' charms. What was he up to? Was he testing Fanny's feelings for him? Was he in fact attracted to the anarchic women, or was he just floundering through his convalescence watching the distorted lantern show of life at Mentone?

25

His nights were again confused by dreams 'of long successions of vaulted, dimly lit cellars full of black water, in which I went swimming among the toads and unutterable, cold, blind fishes; now and then these cellars opened up into sort of domed music-hall places, where one could land for a little on the slope of an orchestra . . .' Conducted by Mme Zassatsky no doubt.

Back in Scotland in April 1874 Stevenson becomes increasingly gloomy, preoccupied with his own condition, and equally with Fanny's apparent ill health. Furnas is convinced that this period represented a crisis in the affair, an explosion. He speculates, convincingly, that an exasperated Fanny extracts from Stevenson a promise to behave himself in future. This raised the question, what indiscretion had he committed? What unspoken line had he crossed when briefly reunited with the object of his sexual anguish? In the days before Christmas Stevenson snatches at an unconvincing redefinition of their relationship: 'I do not know what longing comes to me to go to you for two hours and tell you plainly you have another son. This letter will not speak to you plainly enough; and you must eke it out with what you know of me, Madonna, and you do know that I love you dearly–'. A similarly strained and doomed attempt to redefine their relationship characterises the poems of the period.

Stevenson took to wandering distractedly over the Pentland Hills, presumably scaring the sheep as he regaled them with his views of a foul and unjust universe. He took a break sailing round the Western Isles; a listless tour to the North of England and Wales; tinkering with minor literary projects; taking the line of least resistance and half-heartedly resuming his legal studies; but above all, endless letters to Fanny, and a sense of foreboding as her replies became less frequent.

This foreboding was combined with barely sublimated sexual turmoil judging by the letter in which he reflects on the effect that the Elgin marbles had on him: 'But I can think of these three deep-breasted women, living out their days on remote hilltops, seeing the white dawn and the purple even . . . And think dear, if one could love a woman like that once, see her once grow pale with passion, and once wring your lips out upon hers, would it not be a small thing to die?' Identical expressions of anguish find their way into his poetry.

The dark days of January wreaked further havoc with Stevenson's spirits. In a letter to Fanny he repeats his wish to be mothered by her, the urge to kiss her elusive bosoms apparently having been superseded by the need to be swaddled in them. He quickly abandons the role of wise but troubled counsellor and embraces the challenge of this new relationship. 'O dear mother, I am so pleased, so content, so satisfied . . . and what I want is a mother, and I have one now, have I not? Someone from whom I have no secrets; someone, whom I shall love with a love as great as a lover's and yet more; with whom I shall have all a lover's tenderness and none of a lover's timidity'.

Stevenson seems to be increasingly unhinged as he reports on how he had been sick at heart at the sight of 'horrid women and filthy ragged children' he saw on a walk to Leith. He reflects ruefully on the ominously prophetic title of the last poem he sent to his Madonna. *Nous n'irons plus au bois, helas!* In fact very few letters were to see the light of day as his spirits plummeted during the rain lashed autumn and winter months.

The dark sequence of largely unfinished poems that emerged from this period makes us wonder just how close Stevenson came to taking arms against his own sea of troubles and so ending them. Although the image of him travelling the globe to outwit the man with the sickle is a familiar cliché, it is always assumed that the main threat to his life was illness. Perhaps on occasion the threat was suicide. Although a poseur all his days, these short, dark lyrics are not the bastard children of self-dramatisation. Having long abandoned his religious convictions, he would not have been deterred by thoughts of divine retribution.

Grasping at any excuse to escape from Edinburgh and his increasingly gloomy self, Stevenson hit on the giddy wheeze of a canoeing trip with his friend Walter Simpson. The journey was to spawn *An Inland Voyage*, a book which occupies the territory half-way between a worthy gazetteer charting obscure rivers in the Low Countries, and a bourgeois, picaresque narrative peopled by motley innkeepers, pedlars and random river folk. The voyage was however the starting point of an itinerary that was to culminate in Stevenson meeting Mrs Osbourne at Grez.

# 3 THE ONE ILLOGICAL ADVENTURE

An appendage to a hand organ; an old grizzled lioness; the Queen of Bohemia; a school girl of forty; a brimstone enemy; The Witch Woman; a very rum creature; a sorceress; a Bedlamite; Tiger Lily. Fanny Osbourne was Yoko Ono to Stevenson's John Lennon.

In October 1875 Fanny, desperate to escape Samuel Osbourne, her hard drinking, womanising husband, upped sticks in East Oakland, California, and crossed the Atlantic with her three children. Sustained by the hope of enrolling both herself and her daughter in an art school she finally based the family in Paris. The dream turned sour. Harvey, the youngest child, became seriously ill. The ailing toddler was treated with ox-blood and quinine. Despite these ministrations, or possibly because of them, he died. Desperate for respite from her nightmares, Fanny decided to visit the growing artistic community in Grez-sur-Loing.

The bohemians at Barbizon enjoyed teasing the new arrivals with tales about the wild unpredictable Stevenson cousins, the absent bogie men who on their return might evict the American interlopers with shouts of 'Women be gone!' before chasing them through the Fontainbleau woods with sticks. The rumours and memories have endured; the image of Stevenson, probably drunk, leaping through the French windows to capture the heart of the motherly figure taken unawares while eating her supper. Then the Midsummer Night's Dream of attraction and counter attraction as Fanny, Belle, Louis and

Bob courted and shadow boxed. All the while, Fanny Osbourne would quietly roll her cigarettes musing on the recurrent dream that disturbed her nights. She would wake at the moment her hands plunged into the unmarked grave of her dead son, desperate to turn him into a more comfortable position.

Was it love at first sight? More like love at second sight perhaps as Stevenson transferred his amorous affections from one, unhappily married older woman to another, both mourning the death of a child, both called Fanny, but there the resemblance ends. No more chaste hand-wringing angst, his new love had 'insane black eyes, boy's hands, tiny bare feet and hellish energy'.

It is salutary to think that the first edition of Clayton Hamilton's book *On the Trail of Stevenson*, which, with its demure line drawings, sits sedately on the shelves of most Stevenson aficionados, was withdrawn in 1915 because of the reference to 'immediate and complete union between two affinities'. This gentle euphemism caused untold consternation at the time.

Stevenson wrote no poems during the early days of his new love affair. His creative energies were channelled into prose, sketching, and making love in a canoe left to nose its way unguided into the reeds of the Loing. Sensual moments were savoured with the abandon of a sybarite.

His return to poetry shows the worm of transience gnawing away at any residual spontaneity; he anticipates future states of happiness that, from the moment of their articulation, seem ominously unobtainable.

JA Steuart suggests that Stevenson was also distracted by thoughts of at least two of the mistresses he had left in Edinburgh. One of whom, Margaret Stevenson, 'was the daughter of a builder and carpenter of Aberdeen, and during her acquaintance with Stevenson was employed in Edinburgh. The other woman was a native of a Midlothian village, and, I understand, stood on a somewhat lower social level. Both are reported to have been good looking – the first slender and dark, the second tall, fair and remarkably well built . . . The two knew each other, or at any rate met. One meeting took place near Swanston Cottage while Stevenson was there with his parents; and there was, I am informed, a scene of fury resulting in physical violence.'

Many of the poems that refer to his early relationship with Fanny Osbourne were written retrospectively. They are poignant with nostalgia for past times which cannot be relived, as faded and evocative as the haunting sepia photographs from his time at Grez: members of the artistic, self indulgent commune pose with their cigarettes, or sit on the upturned canoes in the shadow of the bridge. Bob with his splendid striped stockings stares knowingly at the camera. And Bob knew everything about his cousin.

When Stevenson died Bob wrote that the world seemed 'changed and deadened at the loss of him who was my first and best friend.' For his part Louis had referred to Robert Alan Mowbray (Bob) Stevenson as 'the man likest and most unlike me that I have ever met.' (Plate 18) The pair shared secrets all their days, and possibly much more. Before RLS burst into the Hotel Chevillon, and into Fanny's life she had been hankering for Bob who in turn was lusting after Belle.

The subsequent two years represented an often unglamorous courtship, not helped by the receipt of anonymous letters from a blackmailer threatening to tell Sam Osbourne of his wife's new relationship. The macho gold miner still had a claim on her heart. When Fanny eventually returned to America she left her younger lover in a state of emotional collapse.

By the time Stevenson had completed his famous solo journey in the Cevennes, rumours of Fanny's ill health were so strong that he feared that she may already be dead.

The reunion that followed his spontaneous but harrowing voyage across the Atlantic was far from joyous or uncomplicated. Fanny appeared so ambivalent towards him that, in despair, Stevenson took himself off into the wilds with 'the itch and a broken heart'. Both the details and the motives behind this bizarre exploit remain unclear. We do know that he became very ill during the weeks that followed and eventually collapsed only to be saved from death by a passing goat rancher. Claire Harman is convinced that his motivation was in part suicidal.

After their reconciliation, both Stevenson and Fanny became unwell. For his part he was 'a mere complication of cough and bones, much fitter for an emblem of mortality than a bridegroom.' In addition to his habitual symptoms, Stevenson had developed a swollen testicle, irritation of the spermatic cord and an acute skin rash. The shadow of syphilis was to prove an unwelcome guest at the couple's banquet.

It fell to Fanny's sister Nellie van de Grift Sanchez to nurse the strange couple through their various illnesses. The poem *To N.V de G.S.* reveals Stevenson's strong feelings towards his future sister-in-law. Clayton Hamilton also detects a sexually ambiguous note to the relationship, referring to 'the alleged hyper-libido aspect' of his illness.

Stevenson later dedicated *Prince Otto*, his most flawed but most sensual novel, to Nellie, 'I still intend – some how, some time or other – to see your face and to hold your hand.' The poem of dedication provides the reassurance that Nellie will be recognised 'By her blue eye and her black brow /By her fierce and slender look /And by her goodness'.

The central character in *Prince Otto*, Countess von Rosen—an older woman—is described by Stevenson in a letter to Henley as 'a fuck-stress'. While this character would appear to be based more on Fanny than on Nellie, the fact remains that the book is dedicated to the younger sister. In later life, perhaps trying to deflect attention from his feelings for Nellie, he claimed that the Countess was based on Mme Zassetski.

While Stevenson's pen and ink sketch of his new family reclining on a Californian hill captures a rare moment of contentment, (Plate 9) the poems written in the months before his wedding show Stevenson yearning for happier, more settled times. The couple's return to Europe in July 1880 marked an equally restless phase in the relationship. They flitted between Riviera resorts, role played home making in Bournemouth, and generally embarked on what Stevenson called 'a long conversation chequered by disputes'.

Although some of the poems suggest there were happy aspects to these 'conversations', a bleak point came in March 1882: 'I wish to God I or anybody knew what was the matter with my wife . . . I am in the blackness of low spirits tonight, for Fanny has had a sharp relapse, and I have hurt my dog and bust my own knee. We have both been in bed for near a week.'

There is some evidence that during this phase of their life together Fanny miscarried. Stevenson's poem *God gave to me a child in part* is cited as proof, but such is the lack of clarity over the date of composition that it could equally belong to a much earlier period, or indeed, it could just as easily support the rumours that Fanny became pregnant during one of their subsequent voyages.

For almost a century the poem has supported a small cottage industry of speculation. This was fuelled in the 1930's when a young man claiming to be Louis's illegitimate offspring published his memoir *Stevenson, My Father*. The book is now untraceable.

Ian Bell in *Dreams of Exile* discusses rumours that Stevenson did in fact have a child by a blacksmith's daughter. The final verse of the poem with its reference to the persona who at the time felt 'immortal among mortal men' would suggest it was written when Stevenson was still young enough to harbour delusions of immortality.

Hellman, citing Rosaline Masson as his source, maintained that *God gave to me a child in part* postdates the Swanston years. The fact that

Masson was reluctant to identify the woman is interpreted by Hellman as precluding Fanny Stevenson, opening the possibility that there were 'two such children in Stevenson's life'. In one of the more infuriating footnotes in the entire RLS critical canon Hellman confides; 'The name of the woman who, I think, Miss Masson has in mind is known to me. If I am right in my surmise, I quite agree with Miss Masson that the omission of the name is far preferable.

There is logic however in linking the forlorn elegy to an unborn or still born child to the letter that Stevenson sent to Walter Simpson in December 1883; 'I must tell you a joke. A month or two ago there was an alarm: it looked like family. Prostration: I saw myself financially ruined, I saw the child born sickly etc. Then said I, I must look this thing on the good side; proceeded to do so studiously; and with such a result that when the alarm passed off – I was inconsolable.' It is difficult though to imagine the Stevensons sitting 'hand in hand with love' as they day-dreamed about their child's future.

The variant lines from the original manuscript, as published by Roger C Lewis in *The Collected Poems of Robert Louis Stevenson,* introduce a further puzzle:

> Where art thou gone? And where is she?
> Alas! She too has left me, o my child,
> As you I left . . .
> When they told me you were dead
> Forgive me, bright and laughing lad
> Forgive me if my soul was glad.

Indeed, where has she gone, and who is she anyway? If, as Claire Harman suggests, this is Fanny Osbourne, these lines would seem to refer to when she deserted Louis in August 1878 and returned to America leaving Stevenson disconsolate on Euston Station. Subsequently he may have believed that Fanny had died during childbirth which would explain his passionate concern and his manic pursuit of her across America.

The 'she' is just as likely, however, to have been one of the women from Stevenson's past. This interpretation would suggest that the pregnant mother left Stevenson's life, and that on subsequently learning of his infant son's death, his first reaction was relief tinged with guilt and regret. These feelings may well have been rekindled if Fanny thought she might be pregnant, in which case the poem may be a composite conjured by separate events. This is a more likely explanation than the suggestion advanced by Furnas and others, that the poem is merely literary artifice; as if Stevenson, by way of a small diversion from writing about pirates, decided to knock off a poem about a dead or still-born child.

Although it may be a tittle-tattle too far, there has been avid speculation about Stevenson's relationship with his young Swiss-french maid Valentine Roche who was well established in the Stevenson household by the time of the 'I must tell you a joke' letter referred to above. If Valentine had carried Stevenson's child Walter Simpson was one of the few people to whom Stevenson could have hinted at such a development.

Fanny was jealous of Valentine, who like many others, put in long hours nursing her master. Valentine, who remained steadfastly loyal to Stevenson all her days, had reciprocal reservations about Fanny. There was clearly something strange about the relationship; Stevenson enjoyed infantilising Valentine, calling her Joe when she was good and Thomassine when she deserved chastising. On one occasion she dressed up in men's clothes and demanded that Stevenson interview her for a job. Most of the rumours relate to the short period in 1885 when Fanny returned briefly to Hyeres. In her absence Valentine slept by the fire in Stevenson's room, in case he haemorrhaged during the night. That she was not immune to the pleasures of the flesh was shown by the circumstances of her eventual dismissal in the South Seas. 'The usual tale of the maid on board the yacht,' as Stevenson expressed it.

There were of course earlier entries in this compendium of rumours, the blacksmith's daughter was not alone. When a servant in the Jenkins household gave birth to a child called Robert in October 1879, it was said that Stevenson was the father. This particular rumour connects to the hint of blackmail Stevenson mentions in the letter to Henley four months later. However, although the world would probably be a better place if peopled by descendents of RLS, there is no real evidence that a lost literary tribe wanders through the Edinburgh streets.

Stevenson was capable of an emotionally inclusive intensity that embraced friends, family and servants. He could enter imaginatively into the lives of others in romantic and sometimes erotic terms. It is the 'what-if' syndrome. What if Nellie were not my sister in law? What if Belle were not my step-daughter? What if Princess Kaiulani (plate 14) were not so young? What if WE Henley had been born a woman? To express these thoughts in his poetry was an act of bravery, which may also go some way to explaining their complex publishing history.

There is no doubt that Stevenson was at the very least immensely fond of his cousin, Katherine de Mattos (plate 6), who falls into the 'what if' category. Like Valentine, she inspired jealousy in Fanny which culminated in the disgraceful *Nixie* affair. In March 1888 Scribners published a short story by Fanny Stevenson that was unashamedly based on an idea–young poet meets a mad woman on a train–plagiarised from Katherine. Fanny's creative contribution extended no further than substituting the concept of a lunatic heroine with a sprite or nixie. Katherine's champion, WE Henley was livid.

The vitriolic correspondence conducted across the Atlantic by Stevenson does not reflect well on him. Lacking the courage to make a stand, he sides with his wife, cutting himself off from both Katherine and the irascible Henley, who had never been a fan of Mrs Stevenson.

In old age Katharine agreed to contribute to Rosaline Masson's compendium of memories despite being 'a little loathe to write of intimate friends and personal matters'. She declares of Louis and cousin Bob 'No other men nor other women were quite to me what these two were and remained'. Several of Stevenson's poems confirm that he reciprocated the sentiment.

Several commentators have noted how attractive Stevenson was to men in general and gay men in particular. Frank McGlynn lists Andrew Laing, Will Low, John Addington Symonds, Henry James and Edmund Gosse. He also quotes Henley describing Louis as having 'feminine force' and the reply: 'I love you Henley'. This is not to suggest that there was necessarily a conscious sexual attraction between the men. (Incidentally, the inspiration for Long John Silver subsequently felled Oscar Wilde with a blow from his crutch.) Claire Harman and Jenni Calder also discuss the erotic aspect of the Stevenson-Henley friendship and Wayne Koesterbaum takes matters further. In *Double Talk: The erotics of male literary collaboration* he quotes a passage in a letter from Stevenson to Henley in which he seems to be hinting that his feelings for Lloyd are ambiguous: 'Tis a problem. We know what form this craving wears in certain cases'. Koesterbaum also cites a later letter to Henley in which he says of Fanny: 'I got my little finger in a steam press called the Vandergrifter . . . and my whole body and soul had to go through it. I came out as limp as a lady's novel'. Koesterbaum concludes that Stevenson is projecting his wife as a 'literate vagina dentate.'

Still, you have to wonder what emotional storms punctuated the Pacific adventure on which the odd couple embarked in 1888. The fragment *To my Wife* written from the schooner Equator in the following year reveals a huge empathy for Fanny, uprooted and cast into an alien environment as she was. The rural imagery loaded with topographical detail that could equally describe Silverado or Davos, is part of a nostalgic longing rather than a projection into the future. From this point onwards Stevenson looks back, not forwards. In several of his later poems, past lovers feature large.

It is difficult to penetrate the emotional heart of Stevenson's last years. We peer at images of him hanging from a ship's rigging, or at the family assembled outside Vailima studying expressions for clues, and wonder, beneath the posing, posturing and the politics how happy was Stevenson? Was Furnas right when he delivered his verdict on the marriage that, 'They two were as different and functionally complementary as the fungus and the alga in lichen on a sterile rock?' Were Stevenson's own words prophetic when he wrote in *Virginibus Puerisque*, 'In the wedded state a man becomes slack and selfish and undergoes a fatty degeneration of his moral being'?

The whole South Seas period remains a mystery. What drove the Stevensons to cross the world and settle in Samoa? It was wander lust, it was profound restlessness, it was again the hunger of hopeless things. The almost halucigenic tropical experience must have deadened Stevenson's sense of mortality. He had achieved the fame he craved. He was a comparatively rich man. He had achieved reconciliation with his father. He had acquired a startling wife and a ready made family.

An explanation of sorts may be found in the likely diagnosis of his bi polar disorder. Perhaps key decisions, agreeing to buy *The Casco* for example, were made when his hyper mania was at its most intense. Fanny herself seemed to live on a comparable emotional roller coaster. After all Stevenson ruefully observed 'One day I find her in heaven, the next in hell'. On another occasion he described his wife in a letter to Barrie, 'Hellish energy; relieved by fortnights of entire hibernation.'

Not the best recipe for connubial joy. With time they grew used to living with the consequences of their impulsive actions, and adept at exploiting them for creative purposes.

This cycle or more accurately helix, if both partners were subject to the same violent mood swings, had another, simpler dimension. Stevenson was running away. He was hoping to leave his baggage behind, but it caught up with him. He remained haunted by ghosts of former lovers in a distant country.

He also had little sense of who he actually was. Just as in his early years he alternately played Hamlet and Feste, so in the last five or so years of his life he tried on an astonishing number of guises; partriot in exile, patrician, landowner, self appointed quasi governor, a friend to lepers, politician, campaigner, gentleman farmer, consort of endless minor royalty. Host par excellence and latterly the benevolent despot of Vailima, an ever growing haven for relatives and hangers on.

If his marriage to Fanny was essentially difficult his many roles provided him with sufficient distraction from what otherwise may have been, in other less exotic circumstances, a disaster. Perhaps this is why Furnas decided that the balance of power shifted during the Samoan period, 'He changed the rules in the middle'. Ultimately Stevenson seems the stronger partner. The profusion of roles and indeed the physical dimensions of Vailima gave both Fanny and Louis space to be ill separately.

On one occasion even this space proved insufficient. According to Hellman Stevensons' agent, and would be mentor, the unctuous Mr Moors, deciding that his protégé's health could no longer cope with the 'conditions of his household, of chafing at the restrictions and annoyances at Vailima . . . took the first steps towards the purchase of Nassau island as an asylum for his friend . . . Stevenson seems to have decided that there was no chance of his escaping into that solitude where he might enter into more intimate communion with himself.'

Hellman cites both *The Castaways of Soledad* and *The Waif Woman* as proof of his theory that Stevenson's minor fiction provides allegorical insights into the Stevenson marriage.

He may have a point. There is an easy sexuality about *The Beach of Falesa,* with its aura of moral ambivalence, while autobiographical hints can be seen in *The Bottle Imp.* For her part, it has been suggested that Fanny may have had her own reasons for revising her husband's previously abandoned play *The Hanging Judge* with its message of unqualified loyalty to one's spouse. Justice Harlow places love for his wife above an innocent man's life with the words; 'I will defend my wife . . . I will defend her. What do I care for laws? I love my wife! A beast – a senseless beast would do as I do; shall a man do less?' Was Fanny urging Stevenson to show the same commitment?

Significantly Stevenson's reaction to gossip passed on by Moor about an adulterous mutual friend is reminiscent of the disapproving high moral tone he adopted when writing about Burns. *The Strange Case of the Puritan and the Lecher* perhaps.

The fact remains that while some of the later fiction may provide clues about the Stevenson's emotional health, it is through his poetry that we peer into his soul.

We catch small glimpses of their married life together; the problems with servants, ongoing difficulties with Joe Strong, Belle's opium addicted husband , and the challenge of running Vailima, which morphed imperceptibly into a posh shanty town on stilts. Between the white wooden slats we see the Stevensons, man and wife, in their separate sick beds. With an endless capacity for hypochondria, Fanny usually responded to her husband's illness by replicating his symptoms. Her own complaints read like a medical thesaurus: spotted throat, diarrhoea, drain fever, Bright's Disease, aneurism, angina, infected gall bladder, ulcerated bowels; not forgetting her apparent allergy to Stevenson's piano playing.

Like Archie in *Weir of Hermiston* Louis may have 'loved her like a beast and a brute' but the opportunities for physical expression of passion must have been severely limited by their respective illnesses. Perhaps conjuring the past was a source of comfort, a wallow in dreams of old flames. Or did his eye roam for new loves? In *The Teller of Tales* Hunter Davis comments that if in middle-age Fanny eventually lost her desire and Louis retained his, then 'Samoa was not quite the place to be, with all that unsettling flesh around.' McGlyn and Furnas believe strongly that Stevenson was faithful despite the opportunities that presented themselves in the paradise isles. Stevenson nevertheless found the South Seas women most alluring. In June 1891 he writes to Colvin describing the servant girl Faauma, 'a little creature in native dress of course and beautiful as a bronze candlestick, so fine, clean and dainty in every limb; her arms and her little hips in particular masterpieces.' The same letter suggests she had a rival in Java, a laundress, the insides of whose knees, 'is a thing I never saw equalled in a statue.' He subsequently describes how a languid December afternoon is enlivened by the sight of the maid washing his windows 'in a black *lava-lava* with a red handkerchief hanging from round her neck between her breasts; not another stitch; her hair close cropped and oiled; when she first came here she was an angelic little stripling, but she is now in full flower – or half flower – and grows buxom.' The number of lantern slides depicting scantily clad women in Lloyd Osbourne's photographic archive suggests that his interest – and probably that of his step-father – went beyond that expected of the dispassionate Victorian anthropologist (plate 13).

There has been much controversy over Stevenson's attitude towards his step-daughter. He wrote in *An Object of Pity* 'She is my wife's daughter, my secretary, my amanuensis, my woman-Friday on my desert island, my finder of things, my last assistance, my oasis, my staff of hope, my grove of peace, my anchor, my haven in a storm. She's Belle, I suppose'. In a strange passage from the letter to Barrie quoted above he writes, '(Belle) runs me like a baby in a perambulator, sees I'm properly dressed, bought me silk socks, and made me wear them, takes care of me when I'm well, from writing my books to trimming my nails.' Belle morphs into Alison Cunningham, his childhood nurse.

A photograph (plate 16) taken towards the end of his life shows Stevenson tugging reflectively on his moustache as he dictates to Belle. As the mother's star waned under the weight of illness and mental distress, did Stevenson's attitude to Belle shift? Harman suggests that intimacy with Belle 'became more sustaining and comforting to the writer than his marriage'. As is explained in the notes at the end of this anthology, Stevenson's later poems show the two women merged into one entity Was this blurring of boundaries confined to paper? Ironically it was an intentional confusion that Fanny had always encouraged. Claire Harman refers to the 'strangely complicit rivalry' that united mother and daughter. 'With their very similar figures and gypsy colouring, the two women were often mistaken for sisters and both played up to the coquette potential of the situation.' (Plate 10) In the postscript to her biography Harman identifies a grand total of least four men who were shared by Belle and Fanny, emotionally and perhaps sexually.

Katherine Osbourne who married Lloyd in 1896, and was always perceived as vindictive and vengeful by Fanny, alleged in a letter to Phillip Gosse that at one time Belle had begged Stevenson to marry her rather than her mother. The central character in a long abandoned novel *Vendetta in the West* was based on Belle and, according to Frank McLynn, abandoned in strange circumstances. To add a further layer of complexity Stevenson did little to discourage rumours that Belle was his illegitimate daughter by a Moroccan woman.

Katherine places Stevenson's roving eye in a different, even tragic, perspective: In 1923 she wrote to Hellman, 'He walked through the days of his life alone while longing for companionship and supposing again and again he had found it in some one he idealised, but only to end in piercing disappointment. And he lived in a world of his own making, his imagination not only as a child but up to the end of his life. The real world would thrust itself in on his imagining, then were his moments of sorrowful awakening.'

The carefully crafted photograph of the Stevenson family taken on the veranda at Vailima in 1892, rewards scrutiny. There is the surreal Joe Strong with Cocky the parrot on his shoulder; the self-important, posed languor of Lloyd; the distinctly unamused profile of Margaret Stevenson doing her Queen Victoria impersonation; Fanny looking typically grumpy; RLS gazing at Belle who exudes exactly the type of dark sensuality that attracted Stevenson to her mother in earlier days (plate 12).

While many of Stevenson's poems hint at the dark side of his psyche, a cluster of verses capture the passion he felt for his wife. These feelings may have been interrupted by periods of acrimony and illness. They may have had to compete with other loves. The poems though stand as eloquent testimony to the passion that bound Stevenson to his troubled and troublesome soul-mate in a marriage of complementary differences: Fanny squat and swarthy with a man's heart; Stevenson, a drip of water with a strong feminine streak. In *Dark Women* he looks back at life's tribulations and challenges: fighting with his father, fighting against illness and depression, fighting against the sexual anguish of loving Mrs Sitwell, struggling with Fanny's descent into nervous collapse, coming to terms with their unborn children. All counted for nothing, all were washed away; all outweighed by the clasp of a dusky woman.

# THE POEMS

The anthology features poems directly inspired by his sexual passion
for particular women, and in one instance his emotional bond with a
male friend. Included too are occasional poems that set the scene for
the different phases of his emotional life. A small clutch of bleak, short
and often unfinished poems also have their place. Although their
content tends to be loss in general rather than specific romantic
disappointment, the time and place of composition make it highly
likely that one of the triggers for Stevenson's frequent descent into
suicidal thoughts was love lost. Other poems included here are more
concerned with healthy lust and a general celebration of women.

I am not exploring any possible distinction between the personae
in the poems and Stevenson himself. Separated from their various
anthologies and placed together his love poems have an emotional
integrity that is reinforced by the chronology of his various affairs of
the heart. Even the poems that belong to a world of courtly love with a
succession of lost maidens wandering in idyllic valleys, have at their
core the pain and loss that often characterised his relationships.

His early poems should not be dismissed as slightly grown-up
juvenilia or the outpourings of a young man at a difficult phase in his
life. Like everything else that Stevenson wrote, they can be placed on a
spectrum from wonderful to interesting. A large number belong to the
'unfinished' pile. This doesn't matter, nor does the fact that the
'sedulous ape' in Stevenson was unashamedly pillaging styles and

forms from the whole back catalogue of English, Scottish, French and German poetry.

The poems have been arranged to correspond with the three main stages of Stevenson's emotional life. The opening section embraces his adolescence, student days and early manhood. The middle group are mainly concerned with Fanny Sitwell. The final section relates largely, but not exclusively, to Fanny Osbourne.

One problem presented by the chronology of the poems is that while many do what love poetry normally does, namely capture the moment; many seem to exist in parallel time-scales. Stevenson had the capacity to view current events from a future perspective. Will they remember each other? Will their encounters fade and count for little? Will they seem superficial, or doggedly endure as profoundly life-changing experiences? A poem ostensibly rooted in the recent past may in fact be attempting emotional continuity with a love distant in time.

Stevenson acknowledged this complexity in his verse epistle to Charles Baxter

> Most, those love-fruits withered greenly,
>   Those frail, sickly amourettes,
>     How they brighten with the distance
>     Take new strength and new existence
>   Till we see them sitting queenly
>     Crowned and courted by regrets!

Stevenson, with his writer's sense of posterity, felt an obligation both to the future and the past. This presents a problem with some of the later poems. Is Stevenson celebrating Fanny Osbourne or is he validating his past? If the latter, does this detract from the spontaneity of his present love? Is this time-twist a sort of betrayal? Writing paeans to Fanny from a future perspective may indicate dissatisfaction with the present. But more than that, such an approach expresses Stevenson's acute awareness of the transient nature of things, especially human happiness. He consciously uses it as a device that seeds the rapture of the present moment with hope and doubt.

## Part One

# THE SWINGING GAIT OF HARLOTS

## SONG AT DAWN

I see the silent dawn creep round the world,
Here damm'd a moment backward by great hills,
There racing o'er the sea.
Down at the round equator,
It leaps forth straight and rapid
Driving with firm sharp edge the night before it.
Here gradually it floods
The wooded valleys and the meads
And the still smokeless cities.
The cocks crow up at the farms:
The sick man's spirit is glad:
The watch treads brisker about the dew-wet deck:
The light-keeper locks his desk,
As the lenses turn,
Faded and yellow.

The girl with the embroidered shift
Rises and leans on the sill,
And her full bosom heaves
Drinking deep of the silentness.

I too linger and watch
The healing fingers of dawn –
I too drink from its eyes
The unaccountable peace –
I too drink and am satisfied as with food.
Fain would I go
Down by the winding crossroad by the trees,
Where at the corner of wet wood,
The blackbird in the early gray and stillness
Wakes his first song.

Peace, who can makes verses clink,
Find ictus following surely after ictus,
At such an hour as this, the heart
Lies steeped and silent.
Get back to bed,
Girl with the lace-bosomed shift,
O leaning, dreaming girl, I too grow cold,
I do the same.
Already are the sovereign hill-tops ruddy,
Already the gray passes, the white-streak
Brightens above dark woodlands. Day begins.


## My Brain Swims Empty and Light

My brain swims empty and light
Like a nut on a sea of oil;
And an atmosphere of quiet
Wraps me about from the turmoil and clamour of life.

I stand apart from living,
Apart and holy I stand,
In my new-gained growth of idleness, I stand,
As stood the Shekinah of yore in the holy of holies.

I walk the streets smoking my pipe
And I love the dallying shop-girl
That leans with rounded stern to look at the fashions;
And I hate the bustling citizen,
The eager and hurrying man of affairs I hate,
Because he bears his intolerance writ on his face
And every movement and word of him tells me how
    much he hates me.

I love night in the city,
The lighted streets and the swinging gait of harlots.
I love cool pale morning,
In the empty bye-streets,
With only here and there a female figure,
A slavey with lifted dress and the key in her hand,
A girl or two at play in a corner of a waste-land
Tumbling and showing their legs and crying out to me
    loosely.


## You Looked so Tempting in the Pew

> You looked so tempting in the pew,
>     You looked so sly and calm –
> My trembling fingers played with yours
>     As both looked out the Psalm.

Your heart beat hard against my arm,
  My foot to yours was set,
Your loosened ringlet burned my cheek,
  Whenever they two met.

O little, little we hearkened, dear,
  And little, little cared,
Although the parson sermonised,
  The congregation stared.

# Ne Sit Ancillae Tibi Amor Pudori

There's just a twinkle in your eye
That seems to say I *might*, if I
Were only bold enough to try
  An arm about your waist.
I hear too as you come and go,
That pretty nervous laugh, you know;
And then your cap is always so
  Coquettishly displaced.

Your cap! the word's profanely said,
That little topknot, white and red,
That quaintly crowns your graceful head,
  No bigger than a flower,
Is set with such a witching art,
Is so provocatively smart,
I'd like to wear it on my heart,
  An order for an hour!

O graceful housemaid, tall and fair,
I love your shy imperial air,
And always loiter on the stair,
    When you are going by.
A strict reserve the fates demand;
But, when to let you pass I stand,
Sometimes by chance I touch your hand
    And sometimes catch your eye.


# AFTER READING 'ANTHONY AND CLEOPATRA'

As when the hunt by holt and field
    Drives on with horn and strife,
Hunger of hopeless thing pursues
    Our spirits thorough life.

The sea's roar fills us aching full
    Of objectless desire –
The sea's roar, and the white moon-shine,
    And the reddening of the fire.

Who talks to me of reason now?
    It would be more delight
To have died in Cleopatra's arms
    Than be alive tonight.

## Spring Song

The air was full of sun and birds,
　　The fresh air sparked clearly.
Remembrance wakened in my heart
　　And I knew I loved her dearly.

The fallows and the leafless trees
　　And all my spirit tingled.
My earliest thought of love, and Spring's
　　First puff of perfume mingled.

In my still heart the thoughts awoke,
　　Came bone by bone together –
Say, birds and Sun and Spring, is Love
　　A mere affair of weather?


## The Blackbird

My heart, when first the blackbird sings,
　　My heart drinks in the song:
Cool pleasure fills my bosom through
　　And spreads each nerve along.

My bosom eddies quietly,
　　My heart is stirred and cool
As when a wind-moved briar sweeps
　　A stone into a pool.

But unto thee, when thee I meet,
My pulses thicken fast,
As when the maddened lake grows black
And ruffles in the blast.


## DUDDINGSTON

With claws and chirrupings, the woods
  In this thin sun rejoice,
The Psalm seems but the little kirk
  That sings with its own voice.

The cloud-rifts share their amber light
  With the surface of the mere –
I think the very stars are glad
  To feel each other near.

Once more my whole heart leaps and swells
  And gushes o'er with glee:
The fingers of the sun and shade
  Touch music stops in me.

Now fancy paints that bygone day
  When you were here, my fair –
The whole lake rang with rapid skates
  In the windless winter air.

You leaned to me, I leaned to you,
  Our course was smooth as flight –
We steered – a heel-touch to the left,
  And a heel-touch to the right.

We swung our way through flying men,
    Your hand lay fast in mine,
We saw the shifting crowd dispart,
    The level ice-reach shine.

I swear by yon swan-travelled lake,
    By yon calm hill above,
I swear had we been drowned that day
We had been drowned in love.


# Not Undelightful, Friend, Our Rustic Ease

Not undelightful, friend, our rustic ease
To grateful hearts; for by especial hap
Deep nested in the hill's enormous lap
With its own ring of walls and grove of trees
Sits, in deep shelter, our small cottage—nor
Far off is seen, rose-carpeted and hung
With clematis, the quarry whence she sprung,
*O maitre pulchra filia pulchrior.*
Thither in early Spring, unharnessed folk,
We join the pairing swallows, glad to stay
Where, bosomed in the hills, remote, unseen,
From its tall trees it breathes a slender smoke
To Heav'n, and in the noon of sultry day
Stands coolly buried to the neck in green.

# LO! IN THINE HONEST EYES I READ

Lo! in thine honest eyes I read
The auspicious beacon that shall lead,
After long sailing in deep seas,
To quiet havens in pure ease.

Thy voice sings like an island bird
First by the seaworn sailor heard;
And like roads sheltered from life's sea
Thine honest heart is unto me.

# THOUGH DEEP INDIFFERENCE SHOULD DROWSE

To—

Though deep indifference should drowse
The sluggish life beneath my brows,
And all the external things I see
Grow snow-showers in the street to me,
Yet inmost in my stormy sense
Thy looks shall live an influence.

Though other loves may come and go
And long years sever us below,
Shall the thin ice that grows above
Freeze the deep centre-well of love?
No, still below light amours, thou
Shalt rule me as thou rul'st me now.

Year following year shall only set
Fresh gems upon thy coronet;
And Time, grown lover, shall delight
To beautify thee in my sight;
And thou shalt ever rule in me
Crowned with the light of memory.

## DEDICATION

My first gift and my last, to you
I dedicate this fascicle of songs
The only wealth I have:
Just as they are, to you.

I speak the truth in soberness, and say
I had rather bring a light to your clear eyes,
Had rather hear you praise
This bosomful of songs

Than that the whole, hard world with one consent
In one continuous chorus of applause
Poured forth for me and mine
The homage of due praise.

I write the *finis* here against my love,
This is my love's last epitaph and tomb.
Here the road forks, and I
Go my way, far from yours.

## St. Martin's Summer

As swallows turning backward
  When halfway o'er the sea,
At one word's trumpet summons
  They came again to me —
The hopes I had forgotten
  Came back again to me.

I know not which to credit,
  O lady of my heart!
Your eyes that bade me linger,
  Your words that bade us part —
I know not which to credit,
  My reason or my heart.

But be my hopes rewarded,
  Or be they but in vain,
I have dreamed a golden vision,
  I have gathered in the grain —
I have dreamed a golden vision,
  I have not lived in vain.


## Over the Land is April

Over the land is April,
Over my heart a rose;
Over the high, brown mountain
The sound of singing goes.
Say, love, do you hear me,

Hear my sonnets ring?
Over the high, brown mountain,
Love, do you hear me sing?

By highway, love, and byway,
The snows succeed the rose.
Over the high, brown mountain
The wind of winter blows,
Say, love, do you hear me,
Hear my sonnets ring?
Over the high, brown mountain
*I sound the song of spring.*
*I throw the flowers of spring.*
*Do you hear the song of spring.*
*Hear you the songs of spring?*

# THE RELIC TAKEN, WHAT AVAILS THE SHRINE?

The relic taken, what avails the shrine?
The locket, pictureless? O heart of mine,
   Art thou not less than that?
Still warm, a vacant nest where love once sat?

Her image nestled closer at my heart
Than cherished memories, healed every smart,
   And warmed it more than wine
Or the full summer sun in noon-day shine.

This was the little weather-gleam that lit
The cloudy promontories. The real charm was it
That gilded hills and woods
And walked beside me through the solitudes.

That sun is set. My heart is widowed now
Of that companion thought. Alone I plough
The seas of life, and trace
A separate furrow far from her and grace.

# APOLOGETIC POSTSCRIPT OF A YEAR LATER

If you see this song, my dear
    And last year's boast,
I'm confoundedly in fear
You'll be serious and severe
    About the boast.

Blame not that I sought such aid
    To cure regret:
I was then so lowly laid
I used all the Gasconnade
    That I could get.

Being snubbed is somewhat smart,
    Believe, my sweet;
And I needed all my art
To restore my broken heart
    To its conceit.

Come and smile, dear, and forget
   I boasted so,
I apologize – regret –
It was all a jest and – yet
   I do not know.


## As Starts the Absent Dreamer

As starts the absent dreamer, when a train
Suddenly disengulphed below his feet
Roars forth into the sunlight, to its seat
My soul was shaken with immediate pain
Intolerable, as the scanty breath
Of that one word blew utterly away
The fragile mist of fair deceit that lay
O'er the bleak years that severed me from death.
Yes, at the sight I quailed; but, not unwise
Or not, O God, without some nervous thread
Of that best valor, Patience, bowed my head
And with firm bosom and most steadfast eyes,
Strong in all high resolve, prepared to tread
The unlovely path that leads me toward the skies.


## As in the Hostel by the Bridge, I Sate

As in the hostel by the bridge, I sate
Mailed with indifference fondly deemed complete
And (O strange chance, more sorrowful than sweet)
The counterfeit of her that was my fate,

Dressed in like vesture, graceful and sedate,
Went quietly up the vacant village street.
The still small sound of her most dainty feet
Shook, like a trumpet blast, my soul's estate.
Instant revolt ran riot through my brain;
And all night long thereafter, hour by hour,
The pageant of dead love before my eyes
Went proudly; and old hopes, broke loose again
From the restraint of wisely temperate power,
With ineffectual ardour sought to rise

## I DREAMED OF FOREST ALLEYS FAIR

### I

I dreamed of forest alleys fair
    And fields of gray-flowered grass,
Where by the yellow summer moon
    My Jenny seemed to pass.

I dreamed the yellow summer moon,
    Behind a cedar wood,
Shone white on rippling waves of grass
    Where I and Jenny stood.

I dreamed, but fallen through my dream
    In a rainy land I lie
Where wan, wet morning crowns the hills
    Of grim reality.

## II

I am as one that keeps awake
 All night in the month of June,
That lies awake in bed to watch
 The trees and the great white moon.

For memories of love are more
 Than the white moon there above,
And dearer than quiet moonshine
 Are the thoughts of her I love.

## III

Last night, I lingered long without
 My last of loves to see.
Alas! the moon-white window-panes
 Stared blindly back on me.

To-day I hold her very hand,
 Her very waist embrace –
Like clouds across a pool, I read
 Her thoughts upon her face.

And yet, as now, through her clear eyes
 I seek the inner shrine-
I stoop to read her virgin heart,
 In doubt if it be mine-

O looking long and fondly thus,
    What vision should I see?
No vision, but my own white face
    That grins and mimics me.


### IV

Once more upon the same old seat
    In the same sunshiny weather,
The elm-trees' shadows at their feet
    And foliage move together.

The shadows shift upon the grass,
    The dial point creeps on;
The clear sun shines, the loiterers pass,
    As then they passed and shone.

But now deep sleep is on my heart,
    Deep sleep and perfect rest.
Hope's flutterings now disturb no more
    The quiet of my breast.


# I Wrote Her Name in Snow Last Year

I wrote her name in snow last year
And thought to grave my love in stone;
She spoke three words, the sun broke forth,
And lo! both love and snow were gone.

## Love's Vicissitudes

As Love and Hope together
  Walk by me for a while,
Link-armed the ways they travel
  For many a pleasant mile –
Link-armed and dumb they travel,
  They sing not, but they smile.

Hope leaving, Love commences
  To practise on the lute;
And as he sings and travels
  With lingering, laggard foot,
Despair plays *obligato,*
  The sentimental flute.

Until in singing garments,
  Comes royally, at call –
Comes limber-hipped Indiff'rence
  Free-stepping straight and tall –
Comes singing and lamenting,
  The sweetest pipe of all.


## I Sit Up Here at Midnight

I sit up here at midnight,
The wind is in the street,
The rain besieges the windows
Like the sound of many feet.

I see the street lamps flicker,
I see them wink and fail,
The streets are wet and empty,
It blows an easterly gale.

Some think of the fisher skipper
Beyond the Inchcape stone;
But I of the fisher woman
That lies at home alone.

She raises herself on her elbow
And watches the firelit floor;
Her eyes are bright with terror,
Her heart beats fast and sore.

Between the roar of the flurries,
When the tempest holds his breath
She holds her breathing also —
It is all as still as death.

She can hear the cinders dropping,
The cat that purrs in its sleep —
The foolish fisher woman!
Her heart is on the deep.


# LIGHT AS THE LINNET ON MY WAY I START

Light as the linnet on my way I start,
For all my pack I bear a chartered heart.
Forth on the world without a guide or chart,
Content to know through all man's varying fates,
The eternal woman by the wayside waits.

## Part Two

# A LONG DESPAIR

## TO F.J.S.

I read, dear friend, in your dear face
Your life's tale told with perfect grace;
The river of your life, I trace
Up the sun-chequered, devious bed
To the far-distant fountain-head.

Not one quick beat of your warm heart,
Nor thought that came to you apart,
Pleasure nor pity, love nor pain
Nor sorrow, has gone by in vain;

But as some lone, wood-wandering child
Brings home with him at evening mild
The thorns and flowers of all the wild,
From your whole life, O fair and true
Your flowers and thorns you bring with you!

## SWALLOWS TRAVEL TO AND FRO

Swallows travel to and fro,
And the great winds come and go,
And the steady breezes blow,
    Bearing perfume, bearing love.
Breezes hasten, swallows fly,
Towered clouds forever ply,
And at noonday you and I
    See the same sun shine above.

Dew and rain fall everywhere,
Harvests ripen, flowers are fair,
And the whole round earth is bare
    To the moonshine and the sun;
And the live air, fanned with wings,
Bright with breeze and sunshine, brings
Into contact distant things,
    And makes all the countries one.

Let us wander where we will,
Something kindred greets us still;
Something seen on vale or hill
    Falls familiar on the heart;
So, at scent or sound or sight,
Severed souls by day and night
Tremble with the same delight -
    Tremble, half the world apart.

## MUSIC AT THE VILLA MARINA

From some abiding central source of power,
    Strong-smitten steady chords, ye seem to flow
    And, flowing, carry virtue. Far below,
The vain tumultuous passions of the hour
Fleet fast and disappear; and as the sun
    Shines on the wake of tempests, there is cast
    O'er all the shattered ruins of my past
A strong contentment as of battles won.

And yet I cry in anguish, as I hear
    The long-drawn pageant of your passage roll
    Magnificently forth into the night.
To yon fair land ye come from, to yon sphere
    Of strength and love where now ye shape your flight,
    O even wings of music, bear my soul!

Ye have the power, if but ye had the will,
    Strong-smitten steady chords in sequence grand,
    To bear me forth into that tranquil land
Where good is no more ravelled up with ill;
Where she and I, remote upon some hill
    Or by some quiet river's windless strand,
    May live, and love, and wander hand in hand,
And follow nature simply, and be still.

From this grim world, where, sadly prisoned, we
    Sit bound with others' heart-strings as with chains,
    And, if one moves, all suffer,–to that goal,
        If such a land, if such a sphere, there be,
            Thither, from life and all life's joys and pains,
    O even wings of music, bear my soul!

# I Do Not Fear to Own Me Kin

I do not fear to own me kin
To the glad clods in which spring flowers begin;
Or to my brothers, the great trees,
That speak with pleasant voices in the breeze,
Loud talkers with the winds that pass;
Or to my sister, the deep grass.

Of such I am, of such my body is,
That thrills to reach its lips to kiss.
That gives and takes with wind and sun and rain
And feels keen pleasure to the point of pain.
Of such are these,
The brotherhood of stalwart trees,
The humble family of flowers,
That make a light of shadowy bowers
Or star the edges of the bent:
They give and take sweet colour and sweet scent;
They joy to shed themselves abroad;
And tree and flower and grass and sod
Thrill and leap and live and sing
With silent voices in the Spring.

Hence I not fear to yield my breath,
Since all is still unchanged by death;
Since in some pleasant valley I may be,
Clod beside clod, or tree by tree,
Long ages hence, with her I love this hour;
And feel a lively joy to share
With her the sun and rain and air,

To taste her quiet neighbourhood
As the dumb things of field and wood,
The clod, the tree, and starry flower,
Alone of all things have the power.

## LET LOVE GO, IF GO SHE WILL

Let love go, if go she will.
Seek not, O fool, her wanton flight to stay.
    Of all she gives and takes away
The best remains behind her still.

The best remains behind: in vain
Joy may she give and take again,
Joy she may take and leave us pain,
    If yet she leave behind
    The constant mind
To meet all fortunes nobly, to endure
All things with a good heart, and still be pure.
Still to be foremost in the foremost cause,
And still be worthy of love that was.

Love coming is omnipotent indeed,
But not love going. Let her go. The seed
Springs in the favouring Summer air, and grows,
And waxes strong; and when the summer goes
    Remains, a perfect tree.

Joy she may give and take again,
Joy she may take and leave us pain.
    O Love, and what care we?

For one thing thou hast given, O Love, one thing
   Is ours that nothing can remove;
And as the king discrowned is still a king,
   The unhappy lover still preserves his love.


# I AM LIKE ONE THAT FOR LONG DAYS HAD SATE

I am like one that for long days had sate,
With seaward eyes set keen against the gale,
On some long foreland, watching sail by sail,
The portbound ships for one ship that was late;
And sail by sail, his heart burned up with joy,
And cruelly was quenched, until at last
One ship, the looked-for pennant at its mast,
Bore gaily, and dropt safely past the buoy;
And lo! The loved one was not there, was dead.
Then would he watch no more; no more the sea
With myriad vessels, sail by sail, perplex
His eyes and mock his longing. Weary head,
Take now thy rest; eyes, close; for no more me
Shall hope untried elate, or ruined vex.

For thus on love I waited; thus for love
Strained all my senses eagerly and long;
Thus for her coming ever trimmed my song;
Till in the far skies coloured as a dove,
A bird gold-coloured flickered far and fled
Over the pathless water waste for me;
And with spread hands I watched the bright bird flee
And waited, till before me she dropped dead.

O golden bird in these dove-coloured skies
How long I sought, how long with wearied eyes
I sought, O bird, the promise of thy flight!
And now the morn has dawned, the morn has died,
The day has come and gone; and once more night
About my lone life settles, wild and wide.


## ALL THINGS ON EARTH AND SEA

All things on earth and sea,
All that the white stars see,
Turns about you and me.

And where we two are not,
Is darkness like a blot
And life and love forgot.

But when we pass that way,
The night breaks into day,
The year breaks into May.

The earth through all her bowers
Carols and breathes and flowers
About this love of ours.


## FEAR NOT, DEAR FRIEND, BUT FREELY LIVE YOUR DAYS

Fear not, dear friend, but freely live your days
    Though lesser lives should suffer. Such am I,
    A lesser life, that what is his of sky
Gladly would give for you, and what of praise.

Step, without trouble, down the sunlit ways.
  We that have touched your raiment, are made whole
  From all the selfish cankers of man's soul,
And we would see you happy, dear, or die.
Therefore be brave, and therefore, dear, be free;
  Try all things resolutely, till the best,
    Out of all lesser betters, you shall find;
And we, who have learned greatness from you, we,
    Your lovers, with a still, contented mind,
See you well anchored in some port of rest.


## If I Had Wings, My Lady, Like a Dove.

If I had wings, my lady, like a dove
    I should not linger here,
But through the winter air toward my love,
    Fly swift toward my love, my fair,
If I had wings, my lady, like a dove.

If I had wings, my lady, like a dove,
    And knew the secrets of the air,
I should be gone, my lady, to my love,
    To kiss the sweet disparting of her hair,
If I had wings, my lady, like a dove.

If I had wings, my lady, like a dove,
    This hour should see my soul at rest,
Should see me safe, my lady, with my love,
    To kiss the sweet division of her breast,
If I had wings, my lady, like a dove.

76

For all is sweet, my lady, in my love;
　　Sweet hair, sweet breast and sweeter eyes
That draw my soul, my lady, like a dove
　　Drawn southward by the shining of the skies;
For all is sweet, my lady, in my love.

If I could die, my lady, with my love,
　　Die, mouth to mouth, a splendid death,
I should take wing, my lady, like a dove,
　　To spend upon her lips my all of breath,
If I could die, my lady, with my love.

# HER NAME IS AS A WORD OF OLD ROMANCE

Her name is as a word of old romance
That thrills a careless reader out of sleep.
Love and old art, and all things pure and deep
Attend on her to honour her advance,-
The brave old wars where bearded heroes prance,
The courtly mien that private virtues keep,-
Her name is as a word of old romance.
Peer has she none in England or in France,
So well she knows to rouse dull souls [from sleep]
So deftly can she comfort those that weep
And put kind thought and comfort in a glance.
Her name is like a [word of old romance]

# Far Have You Come My Lady From the Town

Far have you come my lady from the town,
And far from all your sorrows, if you please,
To smell the good sea-winds and hear the seas
And in green meadows lay your body down.
To find your pale face grow from pale to brown,
Your sad eyes growing brighter by degrees;
Far have you come my lady from the town
And far from all your sorrows if you please.

Here in this seaboard land of old renown,
In meadow grass go wading to the knees;
Bathe your whole soul awhile in simple ease;
There is no sorrow but the sea can drown;
Far you have come my lady from the town.


# Nous N'irons Plus au Bois

We'll walk the woods no more
But stay beside the fire,
To weep for old desire
And things that are no more.
    The woods are spoiled and hoar,
The ways are full of mire;
We'll walk the woods no more
But stay beside the fire.
    We loved in days of yore
Love, laughter and the lyre.
Ah God but death is dire
And death is at the door –
We'll walk the woods no more.

## GATHER YE ROSES WHILE YE MAY

Gather ye roses while ye may,
   Old time is still a-flying;
A world where beauty fleets away
   Is no world for denying.
Come lads and lasses, fall to play
   Lose no more time in sighing.

The very flowers you pluck today,
   Tomorrow will be dying;
   And all the flowers are crying
And all the leaves have tongues to say,—
Gather ye roses while ye may


## O LADY FAIR AND SWEET

O lady fair and sweet
Arise and let us go
Where comes not rain or snow,
Excess of cold or heat,
To find a still retreat
By willowy valleys low
Where silent rivers flow.
There let us turn our feet
O lady fair and sweet,—
Far from the noisy street,
The doleful city row,
Far from the grimy street,

Where in the evening glow
The summer swallows meet,
The quiet mowers mow.
Arise and let us go,
O lady fair and sweet,
For here the loud winds blow,
Here drifts the blinding sleet.


## LIGHT AS MY HEART WAS LONG AGO

Light as my heart was long ago,
Now it is heavy enough;
Now that the weather is rough,
Now that the loud winds come and go,
Winter is here with hail and snow,
Winter is sorry and gruff.
Light as last year's snow,
Where is my love? I do not know;
Life is a pitiful stuff,
Out with it-out with the snuff!
This is the sum of all I know,
Light as my heart was long ago.


## I SAW RED EVENING THROUGH THE RAIN

I saw red evening through the rain,
Lower above the steaming plain;
I heard the hour strike small and still,
From the black belfry on the hill.

Thought is driven out of doors to-night
By bitter memory of delight;
The sharp constraint of finger tips,
Or the shuddering touch of lips.

I heard the hour strike small and still,
From the black belfry on the hill.
Behind me I could still look down
On the outspread monstrous town.

The sharp constraint of finger tips
Or the shuddering touch of lips,
And all old memories of delight
Crowd upon my soul to-night.

Behind me I could still look down
On the outspread feverish town;
But before me, still and grey
And lonely was the forward way.

## IN THE GREEN AND GALLANT SPRING

In the green and gallant Spring,
Love and the lyre I thought to sing
And kisses sweet to give and take
By the flowery hawthorn brake.

Now is russet Autumn here,
Death and the grave and winter drear,
And I must ponder here aloof
While the rain is on the roof.

# O Now, Although the Year be Done

O now, although the year be done,
　Now, although the love be dead,
　　Dead and gone;
Hear me, O loved and cherished one,
　Give me still the hand that led,
　　Led me on.

# The Rain is Over and Done

The rain is over and done;
I am aweary, dear, of love;
I look below and look above,
On russet maiden, rustling dame,
And love's so slow and time so long,
And hearts and eyes so blindly wrong,
I am half weary of my love,
And pray that life were done.

# All Night Through, Raves or Broods

All night through, raves and broods
The fitful wind among the woods;
All night through, hark! The rain
Beats upon the window pane.

And still my heart is far away,
Still dwells in many a bygone day,
And still follows hope with [rainbow wing]
Adown the golden ways of spring.

In many a wood my fancy strays,
In many unforgotten Mays,
And still I feel the wandering—

[*Manuscript breaks off here.*]

## THERE WHERE THE LAND OF LOVE

There where the land of love,
Grown about by fragrant bushes,
Sunken in a winding valley,
   Where the clear winds blow
   And the shadows come and go,
   And the cattle stand and low
And the sheep bells and the linnets
Sing and tinkle musically.
Between the past and the future,
   Those two black infinities
   Between which our brief life
   Flashes a moment and goes out.

## LOVE, WHAT IS LOVE?

Love—what is love? A great and aching heart;
Wrung hands; and silence; and a long despair.
Life—what is life? Upon a moorland bare
To see love coming and see love depart.

## Soon Our Friends Perish

Soon our friends perish,
Soon all we cherish
Fades as days darken – goes as flowers go.
Soon in December
Over an ember,
Lonely we hearken, as loud winds blow.


## I Who All the Winter Through

I who all the winter through,
Cherished other loves than you,
And kept hands with hoary policy in marriage bed and pew;
Now I know the false and true,
For the earnest sun looks through,
And my old love comes to meet me in the dawning and the
    dew.

Now the hedged meads renew
Rustic odour, smiling hue,
And the clean air shines and twinkles as the world goes
    wheeling through;
And my heart springs up anew,
Bright and confident and true,
And my old love comes to meet me in the dawning and the
    dew.

*Alison Cunningham, Stevenson's nurse.*

'My second Mother, my first Wife,
The angel of my infant life'
*A Child's Garden of Verses*

*Swanston Village 2008*

Stevenson's early affairs were conducted in the hills surrounding the village.

*The Bridge at Grez 2008*

There are hints in several of his poems that RLS and Fanny made love on the river that flowed beneath the bridge.

*Rutherfords Bar Edinburgh 2009*

The only remaining public house where Stevenson drank during his student days and probably entertained women from the Old Town. The interior was recently gutted and turned into a restaurant.

'and when I remembered all that I hoped and feared as I pickled about Rutherfords in the rain and the east wind . . . how I feared I should never have a friend far less a wife . . . and then now — what a change! I feel somehow as if I should like the incident set upon a brass plate at the corner of that dreary thoroughfare, for all students to read, poor devils, when their hearts are down.'

*Letters*

*Fanny Sitwell*

'Remember always that you are my friend, and now, my dearest, beautiful friend, good night to you.'

*Letters*

*Katherine de Mattos, Stervenson's younger cousin*
An anonymous watercolour

'It's ill to break the bonds that God decreed to bind,
Still we'll be the children of the heather and the wind;
Far away from home, O, it's still for you and me
That the wind is blowing bonnie in the north countrie!'
From the dedication to *The Strange Case of Dr Jekyll and Mr Hyde*

'You know very well that I love you dearly, and that I always will.'

*Letters*

*RLS 1880 aged 29 in the year of his marriage.*

*Fanny Osbourne 1880*

Fanny commissioned this studio portrait to send to her prospective father-in-law. The cross around her neck would not have gone unnoticed by Thomas Stevenson still smarting from his son's apostasy.

*Hillside Sketch.*

The previously unpublished sketch by Stevenson captures an idyllic moment on a Californian hillside. The outing with his new family must have been a welcome respite from the complexity and challenges of his life at that time.

*'Belle with a young man'*

The title hints at the teasing ambiguous nature of their relationship. RLS was nearer in age to his step-daughter than he was to his wife. This image was wrongly labelled at an exhibition as a wedding portrait of RLS and Fanny.

*The Family in Sydney*

A family portrait taken in 1890. Belle seems to have inserted herself so as to be as close to Stevenson as possible.

*On the veranda at Vailima*

Again RLS and Belle are physically very close; he seems to be staring at her, Belle for her part exudes a beauty and confidence that contrasts with Fanny sinking into the background. Stevenson's mother seems not to be in the best frame of mind while Joe, with parrot, is presumably waiting for the sun to fall beneath the yardarm.

'A Dusky Maiden'

The photograph from Lloyd's extensive record of the family travels is not untypical of his preferred subject matter. His chosen title has a slightly salacious, exploitative feel to it.

*Princess Kaiulani*

The princess' journey into exile mirrored Stevenson's own, but in reverse. He was very fond of her.

> 'Forth from her land she goes
> The island maid, the island rose,
> Light of heart and bright of face:
> The daughter of a double race
> *O Princess Kaiulani*

*The Critic on the Hearth*

Fanny, lips pursed, as she listens to RLS reading from *St Ives* looks every inch the severe critic.

*RLS dictating to Belle*

The intimate gentleness of RLS dictating to Belle is in marked contrast of the severity of *The Critic on the Hearth* (above). Belle was much more than his amanuensis. Although a familiar image it bears closer investigation, there is something incongruous about the array of phallic revolvers pointing down towards Belle while a small Buddha nestles on the corner of the mantelpiece.

*Mrs Isobelle Strong*

Belle, a handsome woman all her days, became enormously rich in later life. She married an oil tycoon twelve years younger than her who may also at one time have been her mother's lover.

*Cousin Bob*

A previously unpublished photograph thought to be of Bob Stevenson, RLS' cousin.

The image provides a haunting notion of how RLS may have looked had he lived into old age. When Stevenson died Bob wrote that the world seemed 'changed and deadened by the loss of him who was my first and best friend.'

If this anthology raises questions about the identity of Stevenson's lovers, Bob knew all the answers and kept his council to the end.

# LOVE IS THE VERY HEART OF SPRING

Love is the very heart of Spring;
　Flocks fall to loving on the lea
And wildfowl love upon the wing,
　When spring first enters like a sea.

When Spring first enters like a sea
　Into the heart of everything;
Bestir yourselves religiously,
　Incense before love's altar bring.

Incense before love's altar bring,
　Flowers from the flowering hawthorn tree,
Flowers from the margin of the Spring,
　For all the flowers are sweet to see.

Love is the very heart of Spring;
　When Spring first enters like a sea
Incense before love's altar bring,
　And flowers while flowers are sweet to see.

Bring flowers while flowers are sweet to see;
　Love is almighty, love's a King,
Incense before love's altar bring,
　Incense before love's altar bring.

Love's gifts are generous and free
　When Spring first enters like a sea;
When Spring first enters like a sea,
　The birds are all inspired to sing.

Love is the very heart of Spring,
  The birds are all inspired to sing,
Love's gifts are generous and free,
  Love is almighty, love's a King.


## THE CANOE SPEAKS

On the great streams the ships may go
About men's business to and fro.
But I, the egg-shell pinnace, sleep
On crystal waters ankle-deep:
I, whose diminutive design,
Of sweeter cedar, pithier pine,
Is fashioned on so frail a mould,
A hand may launch, a hand withhold:
I, rather, with the leaping trout
Wind, among lilies, in and out;
I, the unnamed, inviolate,
Green, rustic rivers, navigate;
My dipping paddle scarcely shakes
The berry in the bramble-brakes;
Still forth on my green way I wend
Beside the cottage garden-end;
And by the nested angler fare,
And take the lovers unaware.
By willow wood and water-wheel
Speedily fleets my touching keel;
By all retired and shady spots
Where prosper dim forget-me-nots;

By meadows where at afternoon
The growing maidens troop in June
To loose their girdles on the grass.
Ah! Speedier than before the glass
The backward toilet goes; and swift
As swallows quiver, robe and shift
And the rough country stockings lie
Around each young divinity.
When, following the recondite brook,
Sudden upon this scene I look,
And light with unfamiliar face
On chaste Diana's bathing-place,
Loud ring the hills about and all
The shallows are abandoned . . .

## NOW BARE TO THE BEHOLDER'S EYE

Now bare to the beholder's eye,
Your late denuded bindings lie,
Subsiding slowly where they fell,
A disinvested citadel:
The obdurate corset, Cupid's foe,
The Dutchman's breeches frilled below,
Hose that the lover loves to note,
And white and crackling petticoat.
From these, that on the ground repose,
Their lady lately re-arose;
And laying by the lady's name
A living woman re-became.
Of her, that from the public eye
They do inclose and fortify,

Now, lying scattered as they fell
An indiscreeter tale they tell:
Of that more soft and secret her
Whose daylong fortresses they were,
By fading warmth, by lingering print,
These now discarded scabbards hint.

A twofold change the ladies know.
First, in the morn the bugles blow,
And they, with floral hues and scents,
Man their be-ribboned battlements.
But let the stars appear, and they
Shed inhumanities away;
And from the changeling fashion sees,
Through comic and through sweet degrees,
In nature's toilet unsurpassed,
Forth leaps the laughing girl at last.

# I Have a Friend; I Have a Story

I have a friend; I have a story;
I have a life that's hard to live;
I love; my love is all my glory;
I have been hurt and I forgive.

I have a friend; none could be better;
I stake my heart upon my friend!
I love; I trust her to the letter;
Will she deceive me in the end?

She is my love, my life, my jewel;
My hope, my star, my dear delight.
God! But the ways of God are cruel,-
That love should bow the knee to spite!

She loves, she hates:- a foul alliance!
One king shall rule in one estate.
I only love; 'tis all my science;
A while, and she will only hate.

## HERE YOU REST AMONG THE VALLIES, MAIDEN KNOWN TO BUT A FEW

Here you rest among the vallies, maiden known to but a few:
    Here you sleep unsighing, but how oft of yore you sighed!
And how often your feet elastic trod a measure in the dew
    On a green beside the river ere you died!

Where are now the country lovers whom you trembled to be near –
    Who with shy advances, in the falling eventide,
Grasped the tightlier at your fingers, whispered lowlier in your ear,
    On a green beside the river ere you died?

All the sweet old country dancers who went round with you in tune,
    Dancing, flushed and silent, in the silent eventide,
All departed by enchantment at the rising of the moon
    From the green beside the river when you died.

## Part Three

# THE ONE ILLOGICAL ADVENTURE

## MINE EYES WERE SWIFT TO KNOW THEE

Mine eyes were swift to know thee, and my heart
As swift to love. I did become at once
Thine wholly, thine unalterably, thine
In honourable service, pure intent,
Steadfast excess of love and laughing care:
And as she was, so am, and so shall be.
I knew thee helpful, knew thee true, knew thee
And Pity bedfellows: I heard thy talk
With answerable throbbings. On the stream,
Deep, swift and clear, the lilies floated; fish
Through its cool shadows ran. There, thou and I
Read Kindness in our eyes and closed the match.

## THE COCK'S CLEAR VOICE INTO THE CLEARER AIR

The cock's clear voice into the clearer air
    Where westward far I roam,
Mounts with a thrill of hope,
    Falls with a sigh for home.

A rural sentry, he from farm and field
   The coming morn descries,
And, mankind's bugler, wakes
   The camp of enterprise.

He sings the morn upon the westward hills
   Strange and remote and wild;
He sings it in the land
   Where once I was a child.

He brings to me dear voices of the past
   The old land and the years:
My father calls for me,
   My weeping spirit hears.

Fife, fife, into the golden air, O bird,
   And sing the morning in;
For the old days are past
   And newer days begin.

## KNOW YOU THE RIVER NEAR TO GREZ

Know you the river near to Grez,
   A river deep and clear?
Among the lilies all the way,
That ancient river runs today
   From snowy weir to weir.

Old as the Rhine of great renown,
  She hurries clear and fast,
She runs amain by field and town
From south to north, from up to down,
  To present on from past.

The love I hold was born by her;
  And now, though far away,
My lonely spirit hears the stir
Of water round the starling spur
  Beside the bridge at Grez.

So may that love forever hold
  In life an equal pace;
So may that love grow never old,
But, clear and pure and fountain-cold,
  Go on from grace to grace.


# NAY, BUT I FANCY SOMEHOW, YEAR BY YEAR

Nay, but I fancy somehow, year by year
  The hard road waxing easier to my feet;
  Nay, but I fancy as the seasons fleet
  I shall grow ever dearer to my dear.
Hope is so strong that it has conquered fear;
  Love follows, crowned and glad for fear's defeat.
  Down the long future I behold us, sweet,
Pass, and grow ever dearer and more near;

Pass and go onward into that mild land
    Where the blond harvests slumber all the noon,
    And the pale sky bends downward to the sea;
Pass, and go forward, ever hand in hand,
    Till all the plain be quickened with the moon,
    And the lit windows beckon o'er the lea.


## SMALL IS THE TRUST WHEN LOVE IS GREEN

Small is the trust when love is green
In sap of early years;
A little thing steps in between
And kisses turn to tears.

Awhile – and see how love be grown
In loveliness and power!
Awhile, it loves the sweets alone,
But next it loves the sour.

A little love is none at all
That wanders or that fears;
A hearty love dwells still at call
To kisses or to tears.

Such then be mine, my love, to give
And such be yours to take:-
A faith to hold, a life to live,
For loving kindness' sake:-

Should you be sad, should you be gay,
Or should you prove unkind,
A love to hold the growing way
And keep the helping mind:—

A love to turn the laugh on care
When wrinkled care appears,
And, with an equal will, to share
Your kisses and your tears.


## THE PIPER: 'INVENI PORTUM'

Again I hear you piping, for I know the tune so well-
   You that rouse the heart to wander and be free,
Tho' where you learned your music, not the God of song can tell
   For you pipe the open highway and the sea.
O piper, lightly footing, lightly piping on your way,
   Tho' your music thrills, and pierces far and near,
I tell you you had better pipe to some one else today,
   For you cannot pipe my fancy from my dear.

You sound the note of travel through the hamlet and the town;
   You would lure the holy angels from on high;
And not a man can hear you, but he throws the hammer down
   And is off to see the countries ere he die.
But now no more I wander, now unchanging here I stay;
   By my love, you find me safely sitting here;
And pipe you ne'er so sweetly, till you pipe the hills away,
   You can never pipe my fancy from my dear.

## To N.V. de G.S.

The unfathomable sea, and time, and tears,
The deeds of heroes and the crimes of kings
Dispart us; and the river of events
Has, for an age of years, to east and west
More widely borne our cradles. Thou to me
Art foreign, as when seamen at the dawn
Descry a land far off and know not which.
So I approach uncertain; so I cruise
Round thy mysterious islet, and behold
Surf and great mountains and loud river-bars,
And from the shore hear inland voices call.
Strange is the seamen's heart; he hopes, he fears;
Draws closer and sweeps wider from that coast;
Last, his rent sail refits, and to the deep
His shattered prow uncomforted puts back.
Yet as he goes he ponders at the helm
Of that bright island; where he feared to touch,
His spirit readventures; and for years,
Where by his wife he slumbers safe at home,
Thoughts of that land revisit him; he sees
The eternal mountains beckon, and awakes
Yearning for that far home that might have been.

# TO W. E. HENLEY

The year runs through her phases; rain and sun,
Springtime and summer pass; winter succeeds;
But one pale season rules the house of death.
Cold falls the imprisoned daylight; fell disease
By each lean pallet squats, and pain and sleep
Toss gaping on the pillows.

   But O thou!
Uprise and take thy pipe. Bid music flow,
Strains by good thoughts attended, like the spring
The swallows follow over land and sea.
Pain sleeps at once; at once, with open eyes,
Dozing despair awakes. The shepherd sees
His flock come bleating home; the seamen hears
Once more the cordage rattle. Airs of home!
Youth, love and roses blossom; the gaunt ward
Dislimns and disappears, and, opening out,
Shows brooks and forests, and the blue beyond
Of mountains.

   Small the pipe; but O! do thou,
Peak-faced and suffering piper, blow therein
The dirge of heroes dead; and to these sick,
These dying, sound the triumph over death.
Behold! Each greatly breathes; each tastes a joy
Unknown before, in dying; for each knows
A hero dies with him – though unfulfilled,
Yet conquering truly – and not dies in vain.

So in pain cheered, death comforted; the house
Of sorrow smiles to listen. Once again –
O thou, Orpheus and Hercules, the bard
And the deliverer, touch the stops again!

## WITH THOUGHTS REVERENTIAL AND STILLY

With thoughts reverential and stilly
This long correspondence I close;
The union of you and your Billy
Now pledges my pen to repose.

On paper as white as a lily,
In writing as sable as crows,
The thoughts of Uxorious Billy
Were daily sent forward in prose.

The postman, industrious gillie,
Has laboured, but may now repose;
For you and Uxorious Billy
On Saturday part from their woes.

But don't come if tired, dear. Your loving husband Louis

## WHERE IS MY WIFE? WHERE IS MY WOGG?

Where is my wife? where is my Wogg?
I am alone and life's a bog.

When my wife is far from me
The Undersined feels all at sea
RLS

## I Am as Good as Deaf
## When Separate from F.

I am as good as deaf
When separate from F.

I am far from gay
When separate from A.

I loath the ways of men
When separate from N.

Life is a murky den
When separate from N.

My sorrow rages high
When separate from Y.

And all seems uncanny
When separate from Fanny.

## My Wife and I in One Romantic Cot

My wife and I, in our romantic cot,
The world forgetting, by the world forgot,
High as the gods upon Olympus dwell,
Pleased with the things we have, and pleased as well
To wait in hope for those which we have not.

She burns in ardour for a horse to trot;
I pledge my votive prayers upon a yacht:
Which shall be first remembered, who can tell —
   My wife or I?

Harvests of flowers o'er all our garden plot
She dreams; and I to enrich a darker spot,
My unprovided cellar; both to swell
Our narrow cottage huge as a hotel,
Where portly friends may come and share the lot
   Of wife and I.

## MEN ARE HEAVEN'S PIERS

Men are Heaven's piers; they evermore
Unwearying bear the skyey floor
Man's theatre they bear with ease,
Unfrowning caryatides!
I, for my wife, the sun unhold
Or, dozing, strike the seasons cold.
She, on her side, in fairy-wise
Deals in diviner mysteries,
By spells to make the fuel burn
And keep the parlour warm, to turn
Water to wine and stones to bread
By her unconquered hero-head.
Sequestered in the seas of life,
A Crusoe couple, man and wife,
With all our good, with all our ill,
Our unfrequented isle we fill;

And victor in day's petty wars,
Each for the other lights the stars.
Come then, my Eve, and to and fro
Let us about our garden go;
And grateful-hearted, hand in hand,
Revisit all our tillage land
And marvel at our strange eastate.
For hooded ruin at the gate
Sits watchful, and the angels fear
To see us tread so boldly here.
Meanwhile my Eve, with flowers and grass,
Our perishable days we pass:
Far more the thorn observe — and see
How our enormous sins go free —
Nor less admire, beside the rose,
How far a little virtue goes.


## GOD GAVE TO ME A CHILD IN PART

God gave to me a child in part,
Yet wholly gave the father's heart:-
Child of my soul, O whither now,
Unborn, unmothered, goest thou?

You came, you went, and no man wist;
Hapless, my child, no breast you kisst;
On no dear knees, a privileged babbler, clomb,
Nor knew the kindly feel of home.

My voice may reach you, O my dear-
A father's voice perhaps the child may hear;
And, pitying, you may turn your view
On that poor father whom you never knew.

Alas! alone he sits, who then,
Immortal among mortal men
Sat hand in hand with love, and all day through
With your dear mother, wondered over you.


# To K. de M.

A lover of the moorland bare
And honest country winds, you were;
The silver-skimming rain you took;
And loved the floodings of the brook,
Dew, frost and mountains, fire and seas,
Tumultuary silences,
Winds that in darkness fifed a tune,
And the high-riding, virgin moon.

And as the berry, pale and sharp,
Springs on some ditch's counterscarp
In our ungenial, native north —
You put your frosted wildings forth,
And on the heath, afar from man,
A strong and bitter virgin ran.

The berry ripened keeps the rude
And racy flavour of the wood.
And you that loved the empty plain
All redolent of wind and rain,
Around you still the curlew sings –
The freshness of the weather clings-
The maiden jewels of the rain
Sit in your dabbled locks again.


*(Additional lines)*

More human grown, yet more divine
You now outsavour, now outshine,
The golden lamps that rare and far
Along the blue embankments are,
The salty smell of running tides,
The rowan wild on mountain sides,
The silver and the saffron dawn
Across the arched orient drawn.


# KATHARINE

We see you as we see a face
That trembles in a forest place
Upon the mirror of a pool
Forever quiet, clear and cool;
And in the wayward glass, appears
To hover between smiles and tears,
Elfin and human, airy and true,
And backed by the reflected blue.

## TO KATHARINE DE MATTOS AVE!

Bells upon the city are ringing in the night;
High above the gardens are the houses full of light;
On the heathy Pentlands is the curlew flying free;
And the broom is blowing bonnie in the north countrie.

It's ill to break the bonds that God decreed to bind,
Still we'll be the children of the heather and the wind;
Far away from home, O, it's still for you and me
That the broom is blowing bonnie in the north countrie!

## SINCE YEARS AGO FOREVERMORE

Since years ago for evermore
My cedar ship I drew to shore;
And to the road and river-bed
And the green, nodding reeds, I said
Mine ignorant and last farewell:
Now with content at home I dwell,
And now divide my sluggish life
Betwixt my verses and my wife:
In vain; for when the lamp is lit
And by the laughing fire I sit,
Still with the tattered atlas spread
Interminable roads I tread.

## AD SE IPSUM

Dear sir, good morrow! Five years back,
When you first girded for this arduous track,
And under various whimsical pretexts
Endowed another with your damned defects,
Could you have dreamed in your despondent vein
That the kind God would make your path so plain?
*Non nobis, domine!* – O, may He still
Support my stumbling footsteps on the hill!

## SO LIVE, SO LOVE, SO USE THAT FRAGILE HOUR

So live, so love, so use that fragile hour,
That when the dark hand of the shining power
Shall one from other, wife or husband, take,
The poor survivor may not weep and wake.

## A DEARER I DO NOT KNOW THAN JOE

A dearer I do not know than Joe,
A sadder girl has rarely been than Thomassine,
Joe is my friend – so may she always be,
And for Joe's sake that darker Thomassine wants
                                        a true friend in me.

## IF I COULD TELL, IF YOU COULD KNOW

If I could tell, if you could know,
What sweet gifts you give away
When you were kind like yesterday,
I think you would be always so.

## My Love was Warm

My love was warm; for that I crossed
The mountains and the sea,
Nor counted that endeavour lost
That gave my love to me.

If that indeed were love at all
As still, my love, I trow,
By what dear name am I to call
The bond that holds me now?

## To Fanny Stevenson
*Verse for her birthday (1887)*

What can I wish, what can I promise, dear,
To make you gladder in the coming year?
I wish you – if I could promise too! –
A kinder husband than you ever knew.

## To My Wife
*(a fragment)*

Long must elapse ere you behold again
Green forest frame the entry of the lane –
The wild lane with the bramble and the briar,
The year-old cart-tracks perfect in the mire,

The wayside smoke, perchance, the dwarfish huts,
And ramblers' donkey drinking from the ruts: –
Long ere you trace how deviously it leads,
Back from man's chimneys and the bleating meads
To the woodland shadow, to the silvan hush,
Where but the brooklet chuckles in the brush –
Back from the sun and bustle of the vale
To where the great voice of the nightingale
Fills all the forest like a single room,
And all the banks smell of the golden broom;
So wander on until the eve descends,
And back returning to your firelit friends,
You see the rosy sun, despoiled of light,
Hung, caught in the thickets, like a schoolboy's kite.

Here from the sea the unfruitful sun shall rise,
Bathe the bare deck and blind the unshielded eyes;
The allotted hours aloft shall wheel in vain
And in the unpregnant ocean plunge again.
Assault of squalls that mock the watchful guard,
And pluck the bursting canvas from the yard,
And senseless clamour of the calm, at night
Must mar your slumbers. By the plunging light,
In beetle-haunted, most unwomanly bower
Of the wild-swerving cabin, hour by hour...

Schooner 'Equator.'

## At Last She Comes

At last, she comes, Oh never more
In this dear patience of my pain
To leave me lonely as before
Or leave my soul alone again.

## To What Shall I Compare Her

To what shall I compare her,
    That is as fair as she?
For she is fairer – fairer
    Than the sea.
What shall be likened to her,
    The sainted of my youth?
For she is truer – truer
    Than the truth.

As the stars are from the sleeper,
    Her heart is hid from me;
For she is deeper–deeper
    Than the sea.
Yet in my dreams I view her
    Flush rosy with new ruth –
Dreams! Ah, may these prove truer
    Than the truth.

## THE UNFORGOTTEN - 1

In dreams, unhappy, I behold you stand
      As heretofore:
The unremembered tokens in your hand
      Avail no more.


No more the morning glow, no more the grace,
      Enshrines, endears.
Cold beats the light of time upon your face
      And shows your tears


He came and went. Perchance you wept a while
      And then forgot.
Ah me! But he that left you with a smile
      Forgets you not.


## THE UNFORGOTTEN - 2

She rested by the Broken Brook
    She drank of Weary Well,
She moved beyond my lingering look,
    Ah, whither none can tell!

She came, she went. In other lands,
    Perchance in fairer skies,
Her hands shall cling with other hands,
    Her eyes to other eyes,

She vanished. In the sounding town,
   Will she remember too?
Will she recall the eyes of brown
   As I recall the blue?

The glitter of the sunny rain,
   The glint of summer dew
The lad that gazed and gazed again,
   Does she remember too?


## To an Island Princess

Since long ago, a child at home,
I read and longed to rise and roam,
Where'er I went, whate'er I willed,
One promised land my fancy filled.
Hence the long roads my home I made;
Tossed much in ships: have often laid
Below the uncurtained sky my head,
Rain-deluged and wind-buffeted:
And many a thousand hills I crossed
And corners turned – Love's labour lost,
Till, Lady, to your isle of sun
I came, not hoping; and, like one
Snatched out of blindness, rubbed my eyes,
And hailed my promised land with cries.

Yes, lady, here I was at last;
Here found I all I had forecast:
The long role of the sapphire sea
That keeps the land's virginity;

The stalwart giants of the wood
Laden with toys and flowers and food;
The precious forest pouring out
To compass the whole town about;
The town itself with streets of lawn,
Loved of the moon, blessed by the dawn,
Where the brown children all the day
Keep up a ceaseless noise of play,
Play in the sun, play in the rain,
Nor ever quarrel or complain;—
And late at night, in the woods of fruit,
Hark! Do you hear the passing flute?

I threw one look to either hand,
And knew I was in Fairyland.
And yet one point of being so,
I lacked. For, lady (as you know),
Whoever by his might of hand
Won entrance into Fairyland,
Found always with admiring eyes
A Fairy princess kind and wise.
It was not long I waited; soon
Upon my threshold, in broad noon,
Gracious and helpful, wise and good,
The Fairy Princess Möe stood.

## DEAR LADY TAPPING AT YOUR DOOR

Dear lady, tapping at your door,
  Some little verses stand,
And beg on this auspicious day
  To come and kiss your hand.
Their syllables all counted right,
  Their rhymes each in its place,
Like birthday children, at the door
  They wait to see your face.

Rise, lady, rise and let them in.
  Fresh from the fairy shore,
They bring you things you wish to have,
  Each in its pinafore.
For they have been to Wishing Land
  This morning in the dew,
All, all your dearest wishes bring —
  All granted — home to you.

What these may be they would not tell,
  And could not if they would;
They take the packets sealed to you,
  As trusty servants should.
But there was one that looked like love,
  And one that smelt like health,
And one that had a jingling sound
  I fancy might be wealth.

Ah, well, they are but wishes still;
    But, lady dear, for you
I know that all you wish is kind.
    I pray it all come true.


# FROM NUMBER TWO TO ANITA NEUMANN

I see where you are driving, dear,
And haste to meet your views.
The nameless man was Number One-
And here is Number Two's

What special charm shall I select
To honour in the Muse?
Your mind – your heart, Anita! dyed
In early morning blues,
With just a hint of fire to warm
Its cold amoral hues?
Your grey eyes, or your slender hands?
In faith I may not choose!

An angel inexpert, untried,
Lingering as angel's use-
Too nice to wet your perfect feet
In merely earthly dews.
The day shall come-it is not far-
When life shall claim its dues,
And fair Anita to fair love
Her hand no more refuse.

Alas! the rhyme is nearly out
I was so rash to choose!
Anita, with my right goodwill,
Take this of Number Two's.
R L S

## O Princess Kaiulani

Forth from her land to mine she goes,
The island maid, the island rose,
Light of heart and bright of face:
The daughter of a double race.

Her islands here, in Southern sun
Shall mourn their Kaiulani gone,
And I, in her dear banyan shade,
Look vainly for my little maid.

But our Scots islands far away
Shall glitter with unwonted day,
And cast for once their tempests by
To smile in Kaiulani's eye.

## Mother and Daughter

*High as my heart!* — the quip be mine
That draws their stature to a line,
My pair of fairies plump and dark,
The dryads of my cattle park.

Here by my window close I sit
And watch (and my heart laughs at it)
How these my dragon-lilies are
Alike and yet dissimilar.
From European womankind
They are divided and defined
By the free limb and the plain mind,
The nobler gait, the naked foot,
The indiscreeter petticoat;
And show, by each enduring cause,
More like what Eve in Eden was:-
Buxom and free, flowing and fine,
In every limb, in every line,
Inimitably feminine.
Like ripe fruit on the espaliers
Their sun-bepainted hue appears,
And the white lace (when lace they wear)
Shows on their golden breast more fair.
So far the same they seem. And yet
One apes the shrew, one the coquette:-
A sybil or a truant child,
One runs – with a crop halo – wild;
And one, more sedulous to please,
Her long dark hair, deep as her knees
And thrid with living silver, sees.

What need have I of wealth or fame,
A club, an oft-printed name?
It more contents my heart to know
Them going simply to and fro;

To see the dear pair pause and pass
Girded, among the drenching grass,
In the resplendent sun; or hear,
When the huge moon delays to appear,
Their kindred voices sounding near
In the verandah twilight. So
Sound ever; so for ever go
And come upon your strong brown feet:
Twin honours, to my country seat
And its too happy master lent:
My solace and its ornament!


## THE DAUGHTER

*Teuila — her native name — the adorner*


Man, child or woman, none from her,
The insatiable embellisher,
Escapes! She leaves, where'er she goes,
A wreath, a ribbon, or a rose:
A bow or else a button changed,
Two hairs coquettishly deranged,
Some vital trifle, takes the eye
And shows the Adorner has been by.
Is fortune more obdurate grown?
And does she leave my dear alone
With none to adorn, none to caress?
Straight on her proper loveliness
She broods and lingers, cuts and carves,
With combs and brushes, rings and scarves.

The treasure of her hair she takes;
Therewith a new presentment makes.
Babe, goddess, naïad of the grot;-
And weeps if any like it not!

Her absent, she shall still be found,
A posse of native maids around
Her and her whirring instrument
Collected, and on learning bent.
Oft clustered by her tender knees
(Smiling himself) the gazer sees,
Compact as flowers in garden beds,
The smiling faces and shaved heads
Of the brown island babes: with whom
She exults to decorate her room,
To draw them, cheer them when they cry,
And still to pet and prettify.

Or see, as in a looking-glass,
Her pigmy, dimpled person pass,
Nought great therein but eyes and hair,
On her true business here and there:
Her huge, half-naked staff, intent,
See her review and regiment,
An ant with elephants! and how
A smiling mouth, a clouded brow,
Satire and turmoil, quips and tears,
She deals among her grenadiers!
Her pantry and her kitchen squad,
Six-footers all, hang on her nod,

Incline to her their martial chests,
With schoolboy laughter hail her jests,
And pay her in her girded dress
Obsequious obeisances.

But rather to behold her when
She plies for me the unresting pen
And while her crimson blood peeps out,
Hints a suggestion, halts a doubt,
Laughs at a jest; or with a shy
Glance of a particoloured eye
Half brown, half gold, approves, delights
And warms the slave for whom she writes!

So, dear, may you be never done
Your pretty, busy round to run,
And show, with changing frocks and scents,
Your ever-varying lineaments:
Your saucy step, your languid grace,
Your sullen and your smiling face,
Sound sense, true valour, baby fears,
And bright unreasonable tears:
The Hebe of our aging tribe:
Matron and child, my friend and scribe!

## THESE RINGS, O MY BELOVED PAIR

These rings O my beloved pair,
For me on your brown fingers wear:
Each a perpetual caress,
To tell you of my tenderness.

Let – when at morning as ye rise
The golden topaz takes your eyes –
To each her emblem whisper sure
Love was awake an hour before.

Ah yes! an hour before ye woke
Low to my heart *my* emblem spoke,
And grave, as to renew an oath,
*It* I have kissed, and blessed you both.


## About My Fields, in the Broad Sun

About my fields, in the broad sun
And blaze of noon, there goeth one
Barefoot and robed in blue, to scan
With the hard eye of the husbandman
My harvests and my cattle. Her,
When even puts the birds astir
And day has set in the great woods,
We seek, among her garden roods,
With bells and cries in vain: the while
Lamps, plate, and the decanter smile
On the forgotten board. But she,
Deaf, blind, and prone on face and knee,
Forgets time, family and feast
And digs like a demented beast.

## LET BEAUTY AWAKE

Let Beauty awake in the morn from beautiful dreams,
  Beauty awake from rest!
  Let beauty awake
  For Beauty's sake
In the hour when the birds awake in the break
  And the stars are bright in the west!

Let Beauty awake in the eve from he slumber of day,
  Awake in the crimson eve!
  In the day's dusk end
  When the shades ascend,
Let her wake to the kiss of a tender friend
  To render again and receive!


## MADRIGAL

Plain as the glistening planets shine
  When winds have cleaned the skies,
Her love appeared, appealed for mine,
  And wantoned in her eyes.

Clear as the shining tapers burned
  On Cytherea's shrine,
Those brimming, lustrous beauties turned,
  And called and conquered mine.

The beacon-lamp that Hero lit
   No fairer shone on sea,
No plainlier summoned will and wit,
   Than hers encouraged me.

I thrilled to feel her influence near,
   I struck my flag at sight.
Her starry silence smote my ear
   Like sudden drums at night.

I ran as, at the cannon's roar,
   The troops the ramparts man —
As in the holy house of yore
   The willing Eli ran.

Here, lady, lo! that servant stands
   You picked from passing men,
And should you need nor heart nor hands
   He bows and goes again.

## DARK WOMEN

I must not cease from singing
   And leave their praise unsung,
The praise of swarthy women
   I have loved since I was young;
They shine like coloured pictures
   In the pale book of my life,
The gem of meditation,
   The dear reward of strife.

To you, let snow and roses
    And golden locks belong:
These are the world's enslavers,
    Let them delight the throng.
For her of duskier lustre
    Whose favour still I wear,
The snow be in her kirtle,
    The rose be in her hair!

The hue of highland rivers
    Careering, full and cool,
From sable on to golden,
    From rapid on to pool;
The hue of heather honey,
    The hue of honey bees,
Shall tinge her golden shoulder,
    Shall gild her tawny knees.

Dark as a wayside gypsy,
    Lithe as a hedgerow hare,
She moves, a glowing shadow,
    Through the sunshine of the fair.
Golden hue and orange,
    Bosom and hand and head,
She blooms, a tiger lily,
    In the snowdrift of the bed.

Tiger and tiger lily
    She plays a double part,
All woman in the body
    And all the man at heart.

She shall be brave and tender,
　　She shall be soft and high,
*She* to lie in my bosom
　　And *He* to fight and die.


There shines in her glowing favour
　　A gem of darker look,
The eye of coal and topaz,
　　The pool of the mountain brook;
And strands of brown and sunshine,
　　Or threads of silver and snow,
In her dusky treasure of tresses
　　Twinkle and shine and glow.


I have been young and am old,
　　And trodden various ways,
Now I behold from a window
　　The wonder of bygone days,
The mingling of many colours,
　　The crossing of many threads,
The dear and smiling faces,
　　The dark and graceful heads.


The defeats and the successes,
　　The strife, the race, the goal;-
And the touch of a dusky woman
　　Was fairly worth the whole.
And sun and moon and morning
　　With glory I recall;
But the clasp of a dusky woman
　　Outweighed them one and all.

Take, O tiger lily,
   O beautiful one – my soul.
Love lives in your body
   As fire slumbers in coal.
I have been young and am old,
   I have shared in love and strife
And the touch of a dusky woman
   Is the dear reward of life.

## MY WIFE

Trusty, dusky, vivid, true,
With eyes of gold and bramble-dew,
Steel-true and blade-straight,
The great artificer
Made my mate.

Honour, anger, valour, fire;
A love that life could never tire,
Death quench or evil stir,
The mighty master
Gave to her.

Teacher, tender, comrade, wife,
A fellow-farer true through life,
Heart-whole and soul-free
The august father
Gave to me.

## I KNOW NOT HOW IT IS WITH YOU

I know not how it is with you –
    I love the first and last,
The whole field of the present view,
    The whole flow of the past.

One tittle of the things that are,
    Nor you should change nor I -
One pebble in our path—one star
    In all our heaven of sky.

Our lives, and every day and hour,
    One symphony appear:
One road, one garden—every flower
    And every bramble dear.

## I WILL MAKE YOU BROOCHES AND TOYS FOR YOUR DELIGHT

I will make you brooches and toys for your delight
Of bird-song at morning and star-shine at night.
I will make a palace fit for you and me
Of green days in forests and blue days at sea.
It's there that I'll be yours, it's there that you'll be mine,
Where the green leaves rustle and the blue days shine.

I will make my kitchen, and you shall keep your room,
Where white flows the river and bright blows the broom,

And you shall wash your linen and keep your body white
In rainfall at morning and dewfall at night.
It's you shall be the queen, and it's I shall be the king,
When the full stream gushes and the brown birds sing.

And this shall be for music when no one else is near,
The fine song for singing, the rare song to hear!
That only I remember, that only you admire,
Of the broad road that stretches and the roadside fire.
The broad road that wanders, the bare feet that go,
Where the white rain hisses and the loud winds blow.


## WE HAVE LOVED OF YORE
### (To an air of Diabelli)

Berried brake, and reedy island,
    Heaven below, and only heaven above,
Through the sky's inverted azure
    Softly swam the boat that bore our love.
        Bright were your eyes as the day;
        Bright ran the stream,
        Bright hung the sky above.
Days of April, airs of Eden,
    How the glory died through golden hours,
And the shining moon arising,
    How the boat drew homeward filled with flowers!
        Bright were your eyes in the night:
        We have lived, my love -
        O, we have loved, my love.

126

Frost has bound our flowing river,
　　Snow has whitened all our island brake,
And beside the winter fagot
　　Joan and Darby doze and dream and wake.
　　　　Still, in the river of dreams
　　　　Swims the boat of love -
　　　　Hark! chimes the falling oar!
And again in winter evens
　　When on firelight dreaming fancy feeds,
In those ears of aged lovers
　　Love's own river warbles in the reeds.
　　　　Love still the past, O my love!
　　　　We have lived of yore
　　　　O, we have loved of yore.


# THE STORMY EVENING CLOSES NOW IN VAIN

The stormy evening closes now in vain
Loud wails the wind and beats the driving rain,
　　　　While here in sheltered house
　　　　With fire-ypainted walls,
　　　　I hear the wind abroad,
　　　　I hark the calling squalls –
'Blow, blow,' I cry, you burst your cheeks in vain!
Blow, blow,' I cry, 'my love is home again!'

Yon ship you chase perchance but yesternight
Bore still the precious freight of my delight,
　　　　That here in sheltered house

With fire-ypainted walls,
Now hears the wind abroad,
Now harks the calling squalls.
'Blow, blow, I cry, 'in vain you rouse the sea,
My rescued sailor shares the fire with me!'

## VERSE FOR HER BIRTHDAY (1894)

To the stormy petrel:
                    Ever perilous
And precious, like an ember from the fire
Or gem from a volcano, we today
When the drums of war reverberate in the land
And every face is for the battle blacked,
Nor less the sky that, over sodden woods,
Menaces now in the disconsolate calm
The hurly-burly of the hurricane,
Do now most fitly celebrate your day.

Yet amid turmoil keep for me, my dear,
The kind domestic faggot. Let the hearth
Shine ever as (I praise my honest gods)
In peace and tempest it has ever shone.

## TO BELLE STRONG: BIRTHDAY VERSES

My dear and fair, my kind and pretty,
Why come and sue to me for praise?
Why come and tease me for a ditty?
Who are, yourself, my Song of Days!

Yourself the goddess bright that lingers
Anear – and sings and sanctifies,
The days go round between your fingers,
And the hours brighten with your eyes!

Yourself the poem and the poet,
My dear and fair, my bright and sweet,
The days rhyme (though you don't know it)
And the seasons chime, dear, with your feet!

My bright light (and who could oppose you?)
My inexhaustible fount of smiles,
You are the tune that the whole world goes to,
And the brightness of the passing miles!

The beauty and the song of water
The brightness and the blue of air,
I can be happy, my friend my daughter,
So long as you are kind and fair.


## DEDICATION FOR WEIR OF HERMISTON
## TO MY WIFE

I saw rain falling and the rainbow drawn
On Lammermuir. Hearkening I heard again
In my precipitous city beaten bells
Winnow the keen sea wind. And here afar,
Intent on my own. *race* and place, I wrote.
Take thou the writing: thine it is. For who
Burnished the sword, blew on the drowsy coal,
Held still the target higher, chary of praise

And prodigal of censure – who but thou?
So now, in the end, if this the least be good,
If any deed be done, if any fire
Burn in the imperfect page, the praise be thine!


## FIXED IS THE DOOM

Fixed is the doom; and to the last of years
Teacher and taught, friend, lover, parent, child,
Each walks, though near, yet separate; each beholds
His dear ones shine beyond him like the stars.
We also, love, forever dwell apart;
With cries approach, with cries behold the gulph,
The Unvaulted; as two great eagles that do wheel in air
Above a mountain, and with screams confer,
Far heard athwart the cedars.
                    Yet the years
Shall bring us ever nearer; day by day
Endearing, week by week, till death at last
Dissolve that long divorce. By faith we love,
Not knowledge; and by faith, though far removed,
Dwell as in perfect nearness, heart to heart.
                    We but excuse
Those things we merely are; and to our souls
A brave deception cherish.
So from unhappy war a man returns
Unfearing, or the seaman from the deep;
So from cool night and woodlands to a feast
May someone enter, and still breathe of dews,
And in her eyes still wear the dusky night.

# SINCE THOU HAST GIVEN ME THIS GOOD HOPE, O GOD

Since thou hast given me this good hope, O God,
That while my footsteps tread the flowery sod
And the great woods embower me, and white dawn
And purple even sweetly lead me on
From day to day and night to night, O God,
My life shall no wise miss the light of love,
But ever climbing, climb above
Man's one poor star, man's supine lands,
Into the azure steadfastness of death
My life shall no wise lack the light of love,
My hands not lack the loving touch of hands,
But day by day, while yet I draw my breath,
And day by day unto my last of years,
I shall be one that has a perfect friend.
Her heart shall taste my laughter and my tears,
And her kind eyes shall lead me to the end.

# INSIGHTS AND ORIGINS

I am grateful to Roger C Lewis *The Collected poems of Robert Louis Stevenson Edinburgh University Press 2003* for the dating of the poems, likely place of composition, if known, and for many of the insights into their genesis. As far as possible I have used his spelling and layout. For poems that do not feature in his anthology, I have either followed the version printed by Janet Adam Smith in her *Robert Louis Stevenson Collected Poems Rupert Hart-Davis 1950* or reproduced the text from *Unpublished Poems by the Boston Bibliophile Society, vols.1, 11, and 111* in 1916 and 1921.

I have, though, followed the precedent set by Janet Adam Smith by using the following abbreviations to indicate the details of first publication.

Some of the poems are seeing the light of day for the first time since they were published by The Boston Bibliophile Society in a limited edition of 484.

**VE**: Vailima Edition, 1922.

**NP**: New Poems and variant Readings, 1918.

**B.B.S. 1, 11, 111**: Unpublished Poems, The Boston Bibliophile Society

**Edinburgh**: The works of Robert Louis Stevenson, Edinburgh Edition, Vol X1V (Underwoods, Songs of Travel).

**Songs of Travel**: Songs of Travel, Robert Louis Stevenson, London 1896.

**Letters**: The Letters of Robert Louis Stevenson, edited by Bradford A Booth and Ernest Mehew, Yale University Press, 1994.

**Colvin's Letters**: Letters of Robert Louis Stevenson to his Family and Friends, edited by Sidney Colvin, London 1899.

**Three Letters**: Three Letters from Robert Louis Stevenson, 1902, privately printed.

**Sanchez**: The life of Mrs Robert Louis Stevenson, Nellie Van de Grift Sanchez, Chatto and Windus, 1920.

**J & H**: The Strange case of Dr Jekyll and Mr Hyde, Robert Louis Stevenson, London 1886.

**R.L.S. Teuila**: R.L.S. Teuila privately printed, 1899. 'Being fugitive verses and lines by Robert Louis Stevenson now first collected' by Isobel Strong.

**JAS**: Robert Louis Stevenson Collected Poems, edited, with an Introduction and Notes by Janet Adam Smith, London 1950.

**Gosse**: Biographical Notes on the Writings of Robert Louis Stevenson, privately printed, 1908.

**Hellman**: The True Stevenson A Study in Clarification, George S Hellman, Boston 1926.

**Memories**: Memories of Vailima, Isobel Strong and Lloyd Osbourne (1922 edition).

**Johnstone**: Robert Louis Stevenson in The Pacific, Arthur Johnstone, London 1905.

**Weir of Hermiston**: Weir of Hermiston, Robert Louis Stevenson, London 1896.

**Three Short Poems**: Privately printed, London 1898.

**Thistle**: Works of Robert Louis Stevenson, Thistle Edition, New York 1902.

## *Part One*

# THE SWINGING GAIT OF HARLOTS

**Song At Dawn** *August 1870 Swanston VE*
**My Brain Swims Empty and Light** *1870 Edinburgh VE*
Anyone who ignores these notes and rushes to get a sense of the poems themselves may feel cheated by the first two in the anthology. While they include small cameos of women and girls variously leaning their bosoms on the window sills of Swanston cottages or playing self-absorbedly on waste land among the Old Town tenements they are not love poems. The second begins oddly with a strained comparison between Stevenson's brain and 'a nut on a sea of oil' as he plunders references from his already doomed career as an engineer. However, these two poems provide the perfect visual context for the two main arenas where the dramas of his early love were enacted.

He eyes the well endowed wench in the window, the dallying shop girl with rounded stern and the 'slavey with lifted dress and the key in her hand'. The fresh-smelling dew and the lamplit twilight conjure possibility and the promise of seduction. What better way to introduce an anthology of love poetry than with an evocation of the sheer sense of joyous expectation and the conviction that the next few hours will bring something special?

The remaining twenty or so poems in this section all belonging to the years between 1870 and 1873, have been organised according to their emotional chronology rather than strict adherence to any assumed month and year of composition. Although Stevenson may have indicated a preferred sequence for particular clusters of poems which are reproduced in this section, I have to an extent reorganised them, and interpolated other poems to provide a sense of thematic unity. This means that poems of flirtation are followed by poems of passion and parting, and then by memories that are variously painful, pleasurable or indifferent.

**You Looked so Tempting in the Pew** *Edinburgh B.B.S. 1*
It is not surprising that the congregation stared; their hands were touching, they were playing footsie, his arm was pressed against her breast, her ringlets brushed his cheek.

**Ne Sit Ancillae Tibi Amor Pudari** *1872 B.B.S. 11*
(Be not ashamed of your love for the hand-maiden)
There is speculation about the identity of the servant girl. Hellman maintains that she was Valentine Roche, the Stevenson's Swiss maid with whom he allegedly had an affair; while Roger C Lewis dismisses this notion on grounds of questionable dating, preferring instead Ernest Mehew's theory that she was an employee at the Imperial Hotel in Great Malvern. (Hence the reference to 'your sly imperial air').

**After Reading 'Anthony and Cleopatra'** *Nairn September 1871. B.B.S. 1*
The fact that he has no particular woman in his heart, that he aches with objectless desire, is irrelevant. Ecstatic potential is all. 'The hunger of hopeless things' is an accurate summary of the endless infatuations and subsequent disappointments in love that characterise this stage in his life.

**Spring-Song** *Edinburgh 1871? B.B.S. 1*

The potential is closer to realisation, although he is still sufficiently detached from his own emotions to wonder at the connection between what he feels and the coincidentally glorious weather.

**The Blackbird** *Edinburgh 1871 B.B.S. 1*

Now the passion is real and immediate. The comparatively safe song bird imagery ill prepare us for the shock of the last two lines. 'As when the maddened lake grows black/And ruffles in the blast'. Surprisingly the last powerful verse is omitted from Lewis' anthology

**Duddingston** *Edinburgh Autumn 1871 B.B.S. 1*

Hellman in his Bibliophile Edition observes that on the manuscript of this poem Stevenson, in later life, wrote the words 'the same amour'. Lewis though makes no reference to any comments in the margin.

In these days of global warming it is difficult to think of Duddingston Loch being ice bound.

It is difficult too, not to see Stevenson's face superimposed on Raeburn's iconic skating minister. Unlike the minister our skater is not alone. But who was his companion? Frank McLynn suggests that the girl on the loch may be the 'certain damsel' referred to in letter to Bob in 1870 whom Stevenson was 'very much hit with . . . who shall be nameless. He (his father) detected a nasty overfriendliness towards me on the part of her relations, so when she was taken away by her parents, it was perhaps as well she left when she did.'

Janet Smith in her notes to her *Collected Poems 1950* draws attention to a letter Stevenson later wrote to Mrs Sitwell 'Then I went to Duddingston Loch and skated all afternoon. If you had seen the moon rising, a perfect sphere of smoky gold, in the dark air above the trees, and the white loch thick with skaters, and the great hill, snow-sprinkled overhead! It was a sight for a king'.

In her contribution to *I Can Remember Robert Louis Stevenson*, Mrs. Dale, a family friend, tells us 'Those Stevenson cousins of R.L.S.'s had been brought up in France, and were accomplished skaters, so as there was a long spell of frost that winter we used to meet daily on Duddingston loch, where Bob Stevenson – RLS's chief friend – used to do figure skating beautifully, and looked very picturesque with a heavy crimson silken sash round his waist, and wearing, I think, a velvet jacket.'

This is one of the first sightings of Bob, a major player in the drama of his younger cousin's love life, a recipient of secrets, an agent provocateur and soon to be a diabolic influence in the eyes of Stevenson senior.

Flora Masson in the same book has a related memory; 'Louis Stevenson came and went about them, skating alone; a slender, dark figure with a muffler about his neck; darting in and out among the crowd, and disappearing and reappearing like a melancholy minnow among the tall reeds that fringe the loch.'

Stevenson revisits the sentiments expressed in *Duddingston* in *Apologetic Postscript of a Year Later* and intended that they be published next to each other. Lewis includes the verses as the final part of *Duddingston*.

## Not Undelightful, Friend, Our Rustic Ease *Near Dunblane 1872* B.B.S. 11

This sonnet, part of a sequence, has fuelled speculation that Stevenson was involved with the local quarryman's daughter who may or may not have been the Jennie named in *I dreamed of forest alleys fair:*

'Far off is seen, rose carpeted and hung/With clematis, *the quarry* whence she sprung'

Her identity doesn't ultimately matter, what is more important is the richly coloured sensual sonnet she inspired.

## Lo! In Thine Honest Eyes I Read *Edinburgh 1870 B.B.S. 1*

This and the next poem show Stevenson in slightly more reflective mode. His love, although real and actual, is also seen in the context of what it prefigures in terms of promising a haven and shelter in an undefined future. This approach anticipates some of the later poems inspired by Fanny Osbourne.

## Though Deep indifference Should Drowse *December 1870 B.B.S. 1*

Stevenson takes out an emotional insurance policy as he projects forward into an uncertain and distinctly cold future defined metaphorically by snow showers and thin ice

'Though other loves may come and go

. . . thou

Shalt rule me as thou rul'st me now'.

He was not far wrong with the reference to other loves.

## Dedication *1871 B.B.S. 1*

The affair concludes with a literal parting of the ways. There is a finality, 'a finis here against my love' that leaves no room for regret, pleasurable recollection or nostalgic longing. Most of the remaining poems in this section are concerned with precisely these emotions.

## St. Martin's Summer *1871 B.B.S. 1*

The first lines combine two of the most recurrent images in Stevenson's love poetry; birds and the sea. In common with several other poems in this anthology, the inspiration is a fleeting memory that comes unbidden. On this occasion the memory is welcome, although there is something of an epitaph about the concluding lines.

'I have dreamed a golden vision,

I have not lived in vain'

## Over the Land is April *B.B.S. 11*

Hellman, who first published the poem, notes that while the hand-writing suggests that it belongs to the time when Stevenson was looking forward to joining Fanny Osbourne in America, the imagery and the references to the 'high brown mountain' in particular, suggest it is a reworking of an earlier poem. However Stevenson frequently recycled earlier abandoned poems, lopping off failed lines and grafting the stump onto the fresh flesh of his latest affair.

As the task is unfinished the reader has the small luxury of choosing between the four possible variants of the last line.

In the next group of poems the recollection is far from pleasurable. They provide an insight into one of the bleakest periods of Stevenson's early years.

## The Relic Taken, What Avails the Shrine? *Swanston 1871 B.B.S. 1*

The underlying disillusion seems manageable although ultimately wrapped in self pity. Stevenson himself commented 'pas mal' in the margin.

## Apologetic Postscript of a Year Later *1872? B.B.S. 1*

The poem is best read aloud. Stevenson has borrowed the tone of restrained bitterness from John Donne. Hellman was the first to link this poem with *Duddingston*

Stevenson seems embarrassed when he revisits the skating poem and its ecstatic final boast of being drowned in love. It was only a figure of speech, a Gasconnade, he claims. Indeed

I apologise – regret –
It was all a jest and – yet
I do not know'

The hint of verbal stumbling conveyed by the dashes serves to highlight his genuine perplexity about the significance of the earlier affair with his skating partner.

### As Starts the Absent Dreamer *B.B.S. 11*

The central image of a steam locomotive bursting from a tunnel, 'disengulphed' to use Stevenson's own coinage is unusual to say the least. No one has reprinted the sonnet since Hellman who argued that the theme is the disillusion of love.

The train conveys the shock of an unbidden and deeply painful memory. The sensation, akin to waking startled from a nightmare, is one that recurs in the early poems. There are references elsewhere to the young Stevenson hanging over the North Bridge near Waverley station watching with envy as an endless succession of strangers set out on their journeys. The sonnet hinges on a contradiction between the decision to embrace his fate with fortitude, and the desperate reality of his loss.

Just as Lloyd after his step-father's death was to become obsessed with motor cars so Stevenson's fascination with steam engines and railways was to find expression in *A Child's Garden of Verses, Across the Plains*, his poem, *The Iron Steed* and the rumour that he subsequently started writing a novel based on the conquest of America by the railroad. Given his reservations about Emile Zola it is interesting to speculate about Stevenson's reaction to *La Bete Humaine*, published four years before his own death, in which the steam locomotive becomes a sustained metaphor for sexual power. According to Frank McLynn he considered it a novel 'of the seamy side'.

**As in the Hostel by the Bridge I Sate** *Dunblane 1872 B.B.S. 11*
A similar image of sleeplessness is at the heart of the sonnet. On this
occasion the shock, prompted by the sight of someone who resembled
an old flame, is a 'trumpet blast', a precursor to the endless nocturnal
'pageant of dead love'. Old hopes were broken loose again.

**I Dreamed of Forest Alleys Fair** *Swanston/Princes Street Gardens
1871 B.B.S. 1*
Roger C Lewis provides evidence that this poem in four sections was
to form part of a projected anthology called *Songs and Little Odes*.

Part I has provided a field day for Stevenson gossips. Who was
Jenny, or Jeanie for that matter, depending on how you make sense of
his handwriting?

There is speculation that she is the same girl from nearby Buckstone
who, according to Compton McKenzie, was the somewhat indifferent
recipient of Stevenson's first attempt at editing *A College Magazine*; 'the
lady with whom my heart was at the time somewhat engaged, and who
did all that in her lay to break it; and she, with some tact, passed over
the gift and my cherished contributions in silence.'

Parts I, II and III which describe dream disturbed nights are
dominated by images of the moon – mentioned five times – imparting
a translucent, ghostly feel. In part IV the perspective has changed to
one of acceptance and resignation. The evening sun and the shadows
are a prelude to a 'Deep sleep and perfect rest'.

**I Wrote Her Name in Snow Last Year**
Stevenson aspires to a mood of protective indifference towards his
earlier love.

The four lines give rise to the flippant thought that he would have
needed a whole glacier to carve the names of all the women who at
some point claimed his heart.

## Love's Vicissitudes *Edinburgh 1871/2 B.B.S. 1*

Love and Hope strolling together are soon overtaken by 'limber-hipped Indiff'rence'. There is a connection between the false stylised imagery and the falseness of the sentiment. I am not convinced that Stevenson was ever indifferent to any of his loves, no matter how long the passage of time.

## I sit up Here at Midnight *Edinburgh Dec. 1871 B.B.S. 111*

Stevenson looks disconsolately at the rain lashing the window of his comfortable bourgeois prison in Heriot Row and projects himself imaginatively into the lives of others. What must it feel like if your love is in peril on the sea? The poem's impact is partly undermined by the epithet *foolish* applied to the fisher woman. It is either ironic or an indication that Stevenson cannot be bothered to bring the poem to an appropriate finish, and dismisses it with an unwarranted condescension. This could be defensive. Perhaps the art of composition has brought home to him the fact that, unlike the anguished watcher, there is currently no one in his life, foolish or otherwise, who would crave his safe return.

## Light as the Linnet on my way I Start *B.B.S. 11*

A similar though less pessimistic thought infuses the poem. Although travelling alone he knows that 'The eternal woman by the wayside waits'. She is about to put in an appearance in the guise of Fanny Sitwell.

# Part Two
# A LONG DESPAIR

With the exception of the last three poems, which despite their later dating, relate to the same period in Stevenson's life, the poems in this section are organised according to their likely date of composition. Many of them have not been republished since their appearance in the three volume Boston Bibliophile limited edition of 484 copies. This is partly for the reasons explored in the introductory essay; they are often unfinished, and bleak in tone, but taken together they give great insight to Stevenson's sense of loss and depression, The most likely cause was his doomed relationship with Fanny Sitwell.

**To F. J. S** *Mentone 15 Nov 1873 Edinburgh Underwoods*
The poem was included in a letter to Fanny and was prefaced with the disclaimer 'here is what I often said in good prose, put into bad verse'. The first three verses published here are not bad verse. Stevenson's subsequent decision however to omit the four verses that follow from *Underwoods* was the right one. They decline into an obscure mix of geological terms and mythology as he strains to find an intellectual paradigm that approximates to his love. That he fails spectacularly is amply shown by the paradoxically unforgettable line 'With Saurians wallowing in fat slime'. Other variant lines are . . . 'Think you I

grudge the seed . . . Broad armed the consummated tree' The strange sexual imagery speaks volumes about Stevenson's own frustration.

The letter surrounding the poem ends 'I send you this rubbish to show you, my dear Amalia (which is the name of your *face*, I have found no name yet for your spirit) that I thought of you. Don't criticise it, for the love of Charity, but remember that it was written by a–an imbecile I was going to day and I'm not much better.'

This original manuscript with its deleted dedication to Claire sent the critics into a spin. The uncharitable theory has it that Hellman conveniently chose to ignore the doodle in the margin in case it contradicted his growing theory about other mysterious women. Roger C Lewis shows his unveiled contempt for the early anthologists 'Their standards of research being as low as they were.' No one, though, has conjectured about the name *Amelia* that Stevenson inexplicably uses here to denote Fanny's face but not her spirit.

The idea behind the lines 'Pleasure nor pity, love nor pain /Nor sorrow, has gone by in vain' is a recurrent theme with Stevenson. Like all lovers he needs to believe that such massive passion must mean something; it must have significance, no matter how well hidden, that transcends present anguish.

**Swallows Travel To and Fro** *Mentone Dec.7th 1873 B.B.S. 1*
The manuscript also carries the name Claire, this time, undeleted. Presumably this is the poem which led Stevenson to comment that opium 'does not make me write a good style apparently, which is just as well lest I should be tempted to renew the experiment; and some verses which I wrote turn out, on inspection, to be not quite equal to Kubla Khan.' Maybe not, but it is an effective, sensual evocation of the ways in which the world serves to connect the separated lovers. It is also an extremely happy poem.

**Music at the Villa Marina** *Mentone Spring 74 B.B.S. 1*

Ironically it is Mme Zassetsky's piano playing that makes Stevenson hanker for the real object of his obsession. Orsino like, he listens to the music of love and self indulgently conjures a fictitious arcadia where he and Fanny Sitwell will live and love, and wander hand in hand. This is the same achingly serene but unattainable country to which he wished to escape with his earlier loves. The image of sitting 'bound with others' heart-strings as with chains,/And, if one moves, all suffer' is a powerful expression of the emotional web in which he felt enmeshed. He had used the image himself the previous month in a letter; 'it is a pity there is no way out of the web – we are all so involved and tied up with others.'

There is further evidence in one of the letters written to Fanny after his return to Swanston that this arcadia is at least adjacent to that self same bourn from which no traveller returns.

'One thing I see so clearly. Death is not the end of joy nor sorrow. Let us pass into the clods and come up again as grass and flowers; we shall still be this wonderful shrinking sentient matter – we shall still thrill to the sun and grow relaxed and quiet after the rain, and have all manner of pains and pleasures we know not of now . . . We make too much of this human life of ours. It may be that two clods together, two flowers together, two grown trees together, touching each other deliciously with their spread leaves, conscious all over of each other's dainty kisses (the wind moving them, as love moves us); it may be that these dumb things have their own priceless sympathies, surer and more untroubled than ours.' (6th June 1874)

**I Do Not Fear to Own Me Kin** *1874 B.B.S. 1*

Despite slightly anomalous dating it seems likely that these verses were effectively commissioned by Fanny after she received the letter quoted above. Stevenson certainly acknowledges her role as transcending that of mere inspirer: 'I hope the verses will please you; as they were written to commission, please tell me what you think unworthy, and I will try to remodel it. They were written very fast in the garden . . .' Apart from any other motivation Fanny was, despite her growing Madonna persona, sufficiently human to enjoy the flattery of having poems written to and about her.

Taken together, the poems provide evidence of Stevenson's sense of loss and his ultimately failed attempts to intellectualise the physical separation and emotional turmoil. If *I do not fear to own me kin* shows him enjoying respite care with his make believe family of flowers in some posthumous idyll, he has other masks to try on.

### Let Love Go, If She Will Go *May 1874 B.B.S. 1*

Presumably the words 'Ah God' written in the margins of the manuscript is not a reflection of Stevenson's own despairing judgement of a flawed poem. Rather it is a spontaneous response on being reminded of a traumatic episode in his life. The poem aspires to an unachievable stoicism, and makes an impact precisely because of the doomed ineffectuality of the Kiplingesque exhortations: 'To meet all fortunes nobly, to endure All things with a good heart, and still be pure.'

### I am Like One That For Long Days Has Sate *London 16th June 1874 B.B.S. 1*

Aspirational stoicism gives way to resigned despair in the final lines of both poems in the double sonnet. The central image of the lone yearning soul looking out to sea for the loved one's return is reminiscent of the foolish fisher woman in *I sit up Here at Midnight*. This time though it is for real. Each and every joyous moment of expectation gives way to bitter crumbling disappointment.

The second sonnet is striking for its surreal description of how

'A bird gold-coloured flickered far and fled over the pathless water waste for me;' before dropping dead at the feet of the waiting lover.

According to the date on the manuscript the poems were composed on the same day that Stevenson wrote to his mother from London. At first chirpy and chatty, 'We had a most sp splendid dinner on real turtle stuffed with straw and other delicacies of the season.' He finally gives in: 'I wonder if you will think this letter funny; to me it seems one of the most humorous things on record. And let me tell you, that I never wrote a letter in lower spirits in my life. I was simply at the bottom of a well when I began and am not quite at the top'. Presumably it was more than the fact of sharing a meal with his father that had induced such melancholy. He must truly have been at the lowest of ebbs if he was unable to maintain the pretence and stop his mother worrying about him.

**All Things on Earth and Sea** *Hampstead October 1874 Three letters*
The naive and bland sentiments form part of a happy letter full of self depreciation and humour. The poem is stripped of all but the simplest imagery of earth, sea, stars and flowers as he seeks to reassure Fanny that his feelings are essentially innocent.

**Fear Not, Dear Friend, But Freely Live Your Days** *London Euston Station autumn 1874*
The same vain of self delusion informs several of the poems of this period. Written in the less than romantic surroundings of the smoking room at Euston Station, the persona is that of an older friend, reflective, supportive and well wishing. Apart from a short burst of hagiography, 'We that have touched your raiment are made whole / From all the selfish cankers of man's soul', the tone is one of selfless magnanimity. He only hopes that she finds a port from the storm. For

a change there is no hint that he would give his eye teeth to join her. He even nobly refers to 'We Your lovers' presumably Colvin and the small band of literary postulants who had previously flocked to worship at her skirts.

### If I Had Wings, My Lady, Like a Dove *Edinburgh 7th Heriot Row November 1874 Letters*

The stance of concerned platonic lover is strained to breaking point. Stevenson skilfully recreates the same paradoxical tension between elegant cerebral hypothesis and underlying lust that was the hallmark of the metaphysical poets in the seventeenth century. It is a great poem but it is not the version he finally included in his letter to Fanny. Concerned lest he is seen as transgressing the rules of engagement he made several changes and omitted the line 'to kiss the sweet division of her breast'. In fact the restrained, mathematical precision of the intended kiss mirrors the earlier reference to kissing 'the sweet disparting of her hair' and prepares the ground for the almost sexual climax of the poem. 'To spend upon her lips my all of breath, If I could die, my lady, with my love'. The implied *petit mort* is a long way from wishing her 'well anchored in some port of rest.'

### Her Name is as a Word of Old Romance *1875? B.B.S. 111*

Fanny is now cast as a courtly love figure in a medieval tapestry. Stevenson uses the rondeau form to impose some sort of structure on his increasingly doomed relationship.

### Far Have You Come My Lady From the Town *Chateau Renard Late August 1875 Letters*

As the rondeaux flow he sends this, and the next poem, to Fanny who is also resident in France. In many ways the elegiac tranquillity is as refreshing as the sea breezes it celebrates. The image, though, of Fanny getting a rapid tan as she lies in the meadow grass has not travelled well.

**Nous N'irons Plus au Bois** *Chateau Renard late August 1875 Letters*
The sentiments anticipate those he will later write to his wife in which he anticipates a fond old age with the two of them cuddled up by the fireside. Here the mood is less optimistic as the couple 'weep for old desire / And things that are no more'.

**Gather Ye Roses While Ye May** *France 1875? B.B.S. 111*
It is easy to see why Stevenson was tempted to revisit Herrick's poem as he senses his relationship with Mrs. Sitwell slipping away. His adaptation is more urgent, less wistful than the original.

**O Lady Fair and Sweet** *1875 B.B.S. 111*
Noble and wistful concerns for Fanny give way to chilling intimations of loss. The rondeau form provides the link with the poems written in France. The now familiar invitation to retreat into an utopia of willowy valleys and silently flowing rivers is rendered meaningless by the inescapable, intrusive reality of the doleful city and the grimy street. The insistent beat of the last two lines reinforces the illusory nature of the shared dream. 'For here the loud winds blow / Here drifts the blinding sleet'.

**Light as My Heart was Long Ago** *1875 B.B.S. 111*
The descent continues. The Shakespearian echoes are at odds with the most facile of rhymes that see 'rough' paired with 'gruff'. It may be special pleading for a poor poem that was presumably not meant to see the light of day, but we are certainly left with a sense of Stevenson in despair quite unable to shape his anguish into words. 'Life is a pitiful stuff, out with It —' And then what? He snatches for a metaphor and then gives up, seeking respite from the failure of words by sticking a

pinch of tobacco up his nose. 'Out with the snuff!' A self- deprecatory acknowledgement that there is, actually, little point in anything. It is worth remembering that no matter how strong his inclination to screw up the poem, he didn't. It stayed in his notebook until Hellmann came rummaging through the literary left-overs.

### I Saw Red Evening Through The Rain *1875 B.B.S. 111*
The title alone is sufficient reason for its survival. Although Janet Adam Smith thought it worthy of inclusion in her 1950 anthology, Roger Lewis omits it from *The Collected Poems*. While obviously unfinished, the verses being variants of each other, it has an impressively bleak feel to it. If I were to exercise editor's prerogative, I suggest that all that can be said is said in the first two verses.

### In the Green and Gallant Spring *1875 B.B.S. 1*
The poem starts well and ends badly. The final couplet is cringe making. Stevenson is in a suicidal state of mind.

### O Now, Although the Year be Done *1875 B.B.S. 1*
The fragment is a harrowing vignette. The plea at the heart of the poem echoes the psalmists. We hold out no great hopes of 'the loved and cherished one' stretching out her hand to the damned soul before the pit closes round him. There may also be an intentional bitter ambiguity in the last line.

### The Rain is Over and Done *1876? B.B.S. 111*
If birds and woodlands are Stevenson's preferred symbols for life's promise, then rain and wind represent the snuffing out of hope. Living in Edinburgh, they were in any case his constant unwanted companions. Wearied resignation has come on the back of emotional exhaustion. That the rain has finally stopped is small comfort, he is beyond feeling anything and prays that life were done.

**All Night Through, Raves or Broods** *1876 B.B.S. 111*

The rain is back on with a vengeance. It lashes the windows and the wind shrieks in the trees. He tugs frantically at the hands of the clock and strives to roll back the seasons to be with his love again. In some ways the most articulately poignant line is the one added by his first editor: 'manuscript breaks off here' Stevenson did not just loose interest or open the door to a man from Porlock; the effort was too great, the pain unbearable. He just gave up.

**There Where the Land of Love** *B.B.S. 111*

Here the increasingly familiar arcadian idyll is seen as no more than a fleeting moment between the 'two black infinities' of non existence.

**Love, What is Love** *March 1876 B.B.S. 1*

Hellman comments that Stevenson's increasing melancholy during the winter of 1876 is reflected in the fact that his letter writing virtually dried up apart from the occasional note to Sidney Colvin, a disconsolate few pages to Mrs Sitwell and a note to Anne Jenkin in which he confesses 'I feel fit for little else besides prayer; I cannot be comforted; my wits are frozen.'

**Soon Our Friends Perish** *1876 B.B.S. 1*

The words 'Eli, Eli, Lama Sabachthani' written in the margins of the manuscript are taken from the gospel according to Mathew 'As a codicil to his emotional crucifixion Stevenson adds, 'And why does the damned wind rave in my ears?'

**I Who All the Winter Through** *February 1876 B.B.S. 1*

After this wrist-slitting sequence comes a breath of spring, literally. The mood of claustrophobic darkness has passed. Hope enters stage left 'as my old love comes to meet me'. One interpretation is that

Fanny Sitwell has again declared her love for him, and his heart soars. Perhaps the mere change in the weather gives him cause to think positively about their relationship again.

The internal evidence in the poem however suggests a different scenario. It isn't Fanny striding across the dew to meet him; it is an earlier love, an old flame. Whether milk-maid, harlot, respectable friend of the family, or friend's sister, we don't know but it is not Fanny. After all, he can tell the false from the true, a hawk from a handsaw. 'I who . . . kept hands with hoary policy in marriage bed and pew' is surely a reference to the caustic circle he endured with Mrs Sitwell, Colvin and the ubiquitous but mercifully absent vicar with his dubious habits. The pew is either the one vacated by 'the incubus' or a reference to the hypocrisy of the church-going rituals that he publicly subscribed to in Suffolk. No wonder his heart 'springs up anew,/Bright and confident and true'.

## Love is the Very Heart of Spring *1876 B.B.S. 111*
The mood of celebration continues. Although the repetitive refrain suggests it would make for a better song lyric than a poem, there is no denying that, for a time at least, the shadows have gone, and the good times are about to roll. Except they don't.

**The Canoe Speaks** *Hyeres 17th March 1884 Edinburgh (Underwoods)*
Snatching at distractions to stop himself going mad Stevenson eventually embarks on his Inland Voyage. The journey gave rise to two impressive poems, if not of love most certainly of celebratory lust, which is not a bad alternative when all is said and done.

Although written several years after *An Inland Voyage*, the subject matter of *The Canoe Speaks* must have its origins in that sleepy river borne adventure. Bizarrely the persona is the canoe itself wending sluggishly through various rustic landscapes. There is a hint of what is to come when the lovers cavorting on the bank are taken unawares by the stealthy craft. Just at the point when our vicarious pleasures are denied, the canoe rounds another bend, and there they are. Undressing maidens 'and swift / As swallows quiver, robe and shift / And the rough country stockings lie / Around each young divinity'.

Several commentators have drawn attention to Stevenson's declared penchant for women's underwear. Henley commented in a letter to Baxter 'Louis has confessed that female underclothing – smocks, hose, garters, drawers – are his fate, and that the noblest sight in the world is a washing'.

One of the rejected variants quoted by Roger Lewis has the even more salacious lines 'Each from her ring of clothes, each she Bare as a flower / And loose their girdle on the grass, / And stepping here, each breathing lass /, From her discarded ring of clothes, / Into the crystal coolness goes.' This is the poem that the editor of *Century* magazine declined '. . . afraid of the 'young person' for whom he is obliged to cater and thought that the poem illustrated would be 'a little rude'. Indeed. In a letter to cousin Bob, surely a connoisseur of these matters, Stevenson referred to the poem as a 'shitty thing'.

*The Century* could not bring themselves to commission a graphic to accompany 'The Canoe Speaks' in case it corrupted the nation's youth; 'as illustrations for the poem would likely be a little rude.' At least the editor of the magazine considered the printing the poem in good faith despite the malicious rumour that the publication of the unseen poems could only have been sanctioned by one of Stevenson's enemies.

**Now Bare to the Beholder's Eye** *Hyeres April 1884 B.B.S. 11*
In a letter to cousin Bob Stevenson says of this poem 'I have another on female underclothes which is my own favourite, as that is about the deepest poetry I have'. We are dealing with corsets and crackling petticoats but the underlying sensuality is the same. This time

there is only one woman divesting herself, but you can't have it all ways.

Although there are no direct references to these heartening episodes in *An Inland Voyage* it is possible to peep between the pages and speculate as to the identity of the young strippers who clearly alleviated the tedium of paddling. We can dismiss the occupants of the frequently sighted floating lavatories where presumably the women were innocently washing, not stepping out of, their under-wear. There are other candidates. At Origny Sainte-Benoite 'Three handsome girls from fifteen to twenty' assume the role of groupies and regale the intrepid travellers with questions. 'The girls were full of little shudderings over the dangers of our journey . . . "It is like a violin", cried one of the girls in an ecstasy'.

Further down the Oise, the weird pair of canoeists attract a gaggle of sightseers who follow along the bank in pursuit 'But the girls picked up their skirts, as if they were sure they had good ankles, and followed until their breath was out . . . the foremost of the three leaped upon a tree stump and kissed her hand . . . "Come back again," she cried and all the others echoed her'.

Finally the Lower Oise yields the following: 'But I prefer to mention a girls' boarding-school, and because we imagined we had rather an interest in it. At least there were girls about the garden; and here we were on the river; and there was more than one handkerchief waved as we went by. It caused quite a stir in my heart'.

Bathing maidens is a theme which Stevenson almost revisited in *Tropic Rain*, published in *Songs of Travel*. Hellman prints the following variant lines that never made the finished version:

'Suddenly pealed and fell, with a sound that beat on the ear
The innocent joys of bathers, the innermost pangs of fear.
And pleased as a girl of the islands stands, with streaming hair,
By the well known pool of the river, when all of the village is there,

And laughs aloud to her mates, and shivers and plunges deep:
The virgin spirit of rain laughed and leaned to her leap.'

*At least in Now Bare to the Beholder's Eye* Stevenson's heart is being stirred by innocent pleasures and is no longer being flayed by Fanny Sitwell.

### I Have a Friend; I Have a Story *1876? B.B.S. 111*
There is however one last throw of the dice. Although the date of composition is unclear the poem does seem to be signalling the end of something. Stevenson is in a mood of spurious and unconvincing magnanimity. He claims to forgive despite the hurt he has endured, and yet the prospect of being the recipient of spite and indeed hate seem cruel indeed. Soon such considerations will seem totally irrelevant as he embarks on the final phase of his emotional journey.

### Here You Rest Among the Vallies, Maiden Known to But a Few *Swanston March 79 Three Short Poems*
The correspondence with Mrs Sitwell continued long after he first set eyes on Fanny Osbourne. The poem was written on the back of a letter to his old flame in which he commented, 'But I am a sad young man at times, and tonight is one of them. It all seems such a waste.'

## *Part Three*

# THE ONE ILLOGICAL ADVENTURE

As many of the poems in this section were eventually published in *Songs of Travel* it has to be assumed that their likely date of composition was between 1888 and 1894. These have been interpolated with poems from other sources including letters.

**Mine Eyes Were Swift to Know You** *Samoa?1888–94? B.B.S. 11*
There is much speculation as to when Stevenson consummated his adulterous relationship with Mrs.Fanny Osbourne. These lines suggest that it was, soon after they met. Although the poem itself dates from a later period, the river where the canoe carrying the lovers nudges into the lilies, before rocking to its own insistent rhythm, is surely the Loing. The same rhythm informs the poem, surely one of the best things he wrote, but which for unfathomable reasons has not been reprinted since its appearance in *New Poems* in 1918.

**The Cock's Clear Voice into the Clearer Air** *Train August 1879 B.B.S. 1*
Although not strictly a love poem, it captures the sheer joy and rapture that Stevenson felt when he left his cramped train compartment and breathed in the fresh, exhilarating air of the American plains from the

precarious position of the carriage roof. What greater pleasure for a risk taking train enthusiast?

Roger C Lewis quotes the letter from Stevenson to Edmund Gosse 'I had no feeling one way or the other, until, at Dutch Flat, a mining camp in the Sierra, I heard a cock crowing with a home voice; and then I fell to hope and regret in the same moment'.

### Know You the River Near to Grez *San Francisco December 1879* *B.B.S. 1* (Plate 3)

Looking back to happier times Stevenson refers to his 'lonely spirit'; there is a small sense of loss even at the point of committing himself to Fanny Osbourne for ever. The loss may of course refer to his fear, recorded by Katharine Osbourne in *Robert Louis Stevenson in California*, that, should his health deteriorate again, he would take part in a death bed marriage.

### Nay But I Fancy Somehow, Year by Year *California 1880?* *B.B.S. 111*

Hellman thought it likely that this poem was among the cluster Stevenson presented to his future bride just before their marriage. He certainly imagines life improving; 'The hard road waxing easier to my feet', and anticipates that he will 'grow ever dearer to my dear'. At one level this is the clichéd hope of all lovers, at another it shows Stevenson perhaps acknowledging that the relationship is not yet all it might be. He retreats to exactly the same idealised land that he conjured when at his most unhappy with Fanny Sitwell. A land 'Where the blond harvests slumber all the noon, / And the pale sky bends downward to the sea'. The final image of the warm distant cottage is one that recurs and which comes to represent a poignantly unobtainable future.

**Small is the Trust When Love is Green** *San Francisco 1880 B.B.S. 1*
Still looking forward, Stevenson sketches a more realistic account of the relationship's likely gestation. As of now, there will be both the sweet and the sour, kisses and tears, sadness and gaiety. The persona prophetically concedes the possibility 'should you prove unkind'. He cannot have fully anticipated the over-protectiveness, the jealousies, lost friendships and destroyed manuscripts that would in part define their future together.

**The Piper** *San Francisco 1880 B.B.S. 1*
While presenting a more optimistic and life affirming view, the poem is not without irony. The sub title *veni portum* is Stevenson's declaration that through Fanny Osbourne he has found an open gate to his own happiness. He declares that his love is stronger than the vagabond lure of the road. He defies the Piper: 'But now no more I wander, now unchanging here I stay'. Well, for a few months anyway.

**To N. V. de G.S.** *Oakland California April/May 1880 Underwoods*
Written when he was gravely ill to acknowledge the debt of gratitude he owed to his future sister in law, the poem is an extended metaphor of the sea captain who carefully circumnavigates an island that both intrigues and frightens him. In a future time when lying beside his wife the captain thinks 'Of that bright island; where he feared to touch'. He lies 'Yearning for that far home that might have been'. A case of what-if, if ever there was. He may well have dictated the poem from his sickbed to Nellie who acted – like Belle in the future – as his amanuensis. There would have been a teasing aspect to the dictation as the impact is at the end. Until the last few lines Nellie would not necessarily have known that the poem was about her. Roger C Lewis uncovered additional lines that were omitted from the published version; 'Happy they/Who land and dwell with thee! For I have seen /Promise in thy refusals . . .' What might Nellie Van de Griff have refused Stevenson?

**To W. E. Henley** *Oakland 1880 Edinburgh Underwoods*
If Orpheus and Hercules were replaced by Eurydice and Hecuba in the
penultimate line, then we could easily accept it as a romantic paean.
All the ingredients are there. The familiar imagery of swallows,
shepherds and seaman. There is even a hint of *petit mort*; 'each tastes a
joy unknown before, in dying'.

**With Thoughts Reverential and Stilly** *Kingussie August 1882 Letters*
After the trauma of watching Bertie Sitwell die, Stevenson sought
respite in Kingussie where he eagerly awaited Fanny's arrival from
Edinburgh. The letter in which this, and the following poem, feature
are accompanied by wonderfully silly pen drawings, one of which
shows a stick man running to embrace a more substantial female
figure, a steam train in the background, and the words:
  DER Meeting
  The fat and lean
  Shall then convene

**Where is my Wife? Where is my Wogg?** *Kingussie August 1882 Letters*
Woggs, aka Bogue, was the Stevenson's dog, presumably the same one
that he accidentally injured in the past (see introduction), and about
whom he wrote at least two highly affectionate poems.

**I am as Good as Deaf** *Kingussie August 1882*
This, the third snatch of verse from the same letter, is also illustrated
by a tiny drawing of a minute figure, arms outstretched, on an outcrop
of rock in the ocean.

**My Wife and I, in One Romantic Cot** *Hyeres 1883–4 B.B.S. 111*
A simple poem which anticipates accruing the pleasing accessories that
should accompany the gentle descent into old age: a horse, a yacht, a

garden and a cellar, all acceptable bourgeois aspirations. Perhaps he should have heeded the adage, 'be careful what you wish for'. They ended up with plentiful horses, sailed in more yachts than you could wave a stick at, and enjoyed a garden stolen from the vengeful jungle. No mention, though, of the 'cannibal black boys' who were to haunt and taunt Fanny, or the semi clad women who would tease and please Stevenson. No mention of the mental breakdowns or illness.

## Men are Heaven's Piers *1883 (?) B.B.S. 11*

Despite the initially strained architectural metaphor the poem finds its best expression in domestic cameos. Stevenson sees himself as his wife's protector and provider. Fanny for her part strives to 'keep the parlour warm, to turn/Water to wine and stones to bread'. The image of Fanny as domestic goddess sits uneasily with her earlier gun toting, raunchy persona.

The reference to them as 'A Crusoe couple, man and wife' is prophetic; despite their later efforts to buy an uninhabited island in the South Seas they never managed to live totally apart from human kind.

Stevenson subsequently remembered the garden at La Solitude in Hyeres with great affection and referred to the plumed gum trees 'as the very skirts of paradise'. With echoes of Tennyson Stevenson invites Fanny into the garden. 'Janet Smith noted that two lines, 'A naked Adam, naked Eve, /Alone the primal bower we weave' had been deleted in an early manuscript. Perhaps, like William Blake and his wife, the Stevensons would wander naked through the flowers and grass. Their pleasure though is cut through with foreboding 'as hooded ruin at the gate / Sits watchful, and the angels fear / To see us tread so boldly here'.

## God Gave to Me a Child in Part *Hyeres (?) 1883 B.B.S. 11*

Because of its importance, this poem has been dealt with extensively in the introduction to this anthology. It has been placed here as, despite its complex genesis, chronology and range of allusions, it seems very likely that Fanny Stevenson's pregnancy was a major factor in its composition.

**To K. de M** *Hyeres 1883–4 (Underwoods) Additional Lines B.B.S. 11* and **Katherine** *Hyeres 1883–4 B.B.S. 11*
Both poems, and the additional lines, feature on the same manuscript and show Stevenson's debt to Keats. Sensual, elemental and haunting, Stevenson's love and admiration for Katherine is in every image. She certainly belongs to the 'What–if' category.

**To Katherine de Mattos Ave!** *Bournemouth 19th May 1885 Colvin's Letters (First Verse) and The Strange Case of Dr Jekyll and Mr Hyde (second verse)*
Although the second verse first appeared as part of the dedication to *The Strange Case of Dr Jekyll and Mr Hyde*, the whole poem, according to Roger C Lewis, was one of several written on napkins for the guests at the Stevenson's wedding anniversary at Skerrivore.

In a letter accompanying the copy of *The Strange Case of Dr Jekyll and Mr Hyde* were the words 'You know very well that I love you dearly, and that I always will. I only wish the verse were better, but at least you like the story; and it is sent by the one that loves you – Jekyll and not Hyde'

Surely the fact that Katherine was the dedicatee for *Jekyll and Hyde* must have rankled with Fanny. Perhaps this small act of defiance reflected his continuing anger at his wife having thrust the first draft into the smouldering hearth at Bournemouth.

**Since Years Ago Forevermore** *Hyeres (?) 1883–4 B.B.S. 1*
The cedar ship and the nodding reeds connect, not only with *An Inland Voyage*, but also the canoe gently rocking beneath the weight of the

lovers on the Loing. The past is a distant country. The image of Stevenson reduced to travelling imaginatively across the atlas spread across his lap is poignant in the extreme. He is treading his own private interminable road.

**Ad Se Ipsum** *Bournemouth(?) 1885 (?) B.B.S. 11*

This is a strange and oddly unconvincing poem. Hellman suggested that Stevenson is reflecting on the state of his marriage. If this is the case, although he seems to be acknowledging his good fortune in being wed to Fanny, he also provides insight into his frame of mind at the time of his marriage. 'Arduous track, despondent vein'. Although Stevenson thanks God for showing him the path ahead, he admits to stumbling footsteps. This is either an expression of pious acquiescence, or an honest admission of his frailty and continuing uncertainty. There is also something contrived about addressing the poem to himself, unless he feels the need to give himself a good talking to at a time of doubt.

**So Live, So Love, So Use That Fragile Hour** *Bournemouth (?) 1885 (?) B.B.S. 11*

The sentiments are recognisably from the same pen that adapted Herrick's *Gather ye rosebuds*. A succinct expression of *carpe diem*. We have no context for the poem beyond Janet Smith's suggestion that it was written soon after the Stevensons moved into their new home by the sea. Presumably Louis is genuinely revelling in the pleasure and undoubted challenge of living with Fanny. A determination to live in the present was, in any case, preferable to contemplating a ripe old age in Bournemouth.

**A Dearer I do not know than Joe** *and* **If I could tell, if you could know** *Bournemouth 1885 (?)*

Hunter Davies in *The Teller of Tales* includes both of these snatches of doggerel as evidence of the flirtatious relationship that Stevenson enjoyed with Valentine Roche, the Swiss / French maid who loyally traipsed after the Stevensons. According to Valentine's account; 'When I came in to him one morning, he was busy writing and hardly looked at me. I felt then that I was in disgrace. After I had attended to his wants and was ready to leave, he handed me a scrap of newspaper wrapper on which he had written 'A dearer I do not know than Joe . . .'

**My Love Was Warm** *Kingussie March 1886(?) B.B.S. 11*
A simple lyric that speaks for itself.

**To Fanny Stevenson Verse for Her Birthday (1887)** *Bournemouth 10th March 1887 JAS*
In contrite mood Stevenson aspires to, but significantly can't promise, to be a kinder husband. What unkindness did he think himself guilty of? Perhaps he knew that the Bournemouth days were about to end and that Fanny was soon to be dragged across the world as he played tag with his demons.

**To my Wife** *(A Fragment) The Schooner Equator 1889 Songs of Travel*
The description of life on board echoes this in a letter to his mother '. . . the incessant uproar of the tropic rain, the dripping leaks, the slush on the floor and the general sense that we are nowhere in particular and drifting anywhere at large . . . Fanny has stood the hardships of this rough cruise wonderfully; but I do not think I could expose her to another of the same.'

The poem breaks off at this point; perhaps the inkwell is dislodged by a squall and tumbles messily across the cabin. Presumably in the final missing part he would have declared his love and gratitude to Fanny.

**At Last She Comes** *Samoa 1888–1894 B.B.S. 11*
The lines could have been written at almost any point during the Samoan years. More of a shout of relief than a poem Stevenson with the desperation of a sick child is relieved when his nurse/mother/ lover finally comes to his bedside. Perhaps she had been digging like a demented beast in the garden or shooing the frogs off the tennis court and didn't hear the forlorn cries.

**To What Shall I Compare Her** *Samoa (?) 1888–1894 (?) B.B.S. 11*
This and the next two poems support the view that during his spells of unhappiness Stevenson looked back with longing to earlier times and earlier loves. The where-is-she-now theme is a variant of the what-if syndrome. He dreams of the troubled woman who was 'the sainted' of his youth 'Flush rosy with new ruth.' The final wish,' Dreams! Ah, may these prove truer / Than the truth' reveal the extent of his present misery. Despite his often declared penchant for dark, dusky women, this past lover was fair in all senses of the word.

**The Unforgotten - 1** *Songs of Travel*
Presumably 'unhappy' in the first line 'In dreams, unhappy, I behold you stand' refers to the woman and not the dreamer. It could of course refer to them both. What are the unremembered tokens she holds in her hand? What small gifts had Stevenson given her? Flowers for Mary the street walker? A scarf for Jenny? A poem pressed in to the hand he brushed in the pew?

**The Unforgotten - 2** *Songs of Travel and B.B.S. 11*
Hellman quotes some variant lines, four of which are here added to the version as printed in *Songs of Travel*.

Stevenson is again fulfilling the promise to remember that was a feature of the poems he wrote in his youth. He is keeping his side of the bargain by maintaining emotional continuity with past lovers.

**To an Island Princess** *Tahiti November 1888 Songs of Travel*
After arriving in Tahiti Stevenson fell ill. As Mehew explains, on
hearing that a white man was unwell, Princess Möe, the widow of a
local dissolute king sent him an island delicacy which, according to
Fanny, worked wonders. The restored invalid was more than happy to
present his saviour with these verses.

**Dear Lady Tapping at Your Door** *Waikiki 1889 Johnston*
This is the first of three poems that show Stevenson's emotional
inclusiveness towards women he met socially in the South Seas.
Although the lines suggest a flirtatious friendship rather than love,
this was always a fine line with Stevenson. It is dedicated to Mrs.
Caroline Bush who lived near to the Stevensons in Honolulu.
Certainly, a nicer thing to find on your doorstep than a note from
the milkman.

**From Number Two to Anita Neumann** *Honolulu 1893 Johnston*
Here is Johnstone's note of explanation; 'Stevenson was a welcome
and privileged guest at the Hon. Paul Neumann's residence while in
Honolulu, and coming in one day, he found Miss Anita Neumann
sitting in a pensive mood over some verses that she had just received.
The novelist at once fell into a pleasant way with her, and requested
the name of her admirer, which she refused to divulge, however. That
afternoon, Stevenson concluded his pleasantry by sending a sheet of
foolscap containing the following lines, wherein the young lady's
admirer is designated as *Number One*, and the novelist as *Number Two*.'

**To Princess Kaiulani** *Waikiki 24th April 1889 Songs of Travel*
Stevenson was hugely fond of the young island princess. At one level
he identified with her because her situation mirrored his. She was
about to leave her homeland to travel Stevenson's journey in reverse.

At another level, Plate 14 shows that she was a truly beautiful young woman who belonged to a different planet from the hypochondriac and increasingly weather beaten Fanny.

Janet Smith quotes from Stevenson's notes; 'When she comes to my land and her fathers and the rain beats upon the window (as I fear it will) let her look at this page; it will be like a weed gathered and pressed at home; and she will remember her own islands and the shadow of the mighty tree; and she will hear the peacocks screaming in the dusk and the wind blowing in the palms; and she will think of her father sitting there alone.'

Alanna Knight in *RLS in the South Seas* includes the following information 'Kaiulani returned to Hawaii in November 1897 her health shattered by Britain's climate. Stevenson was dead and she survived him by less than five years, dying in March 1899, aged 24. She lay in state dressed in white, on a purple velvet pall covered by the royal cloak of yellow feathers.'

**Mother and Daughter** *Vailima January 1893 R.L.S. Teuila*
In her memoir Isobel Strong mentions that Stevenson wrote *Mother and Daughter* when he was recovering from two haemorrhages, 'He generally fills in his convalescence with poetry, today he read us some beautiful verses . . .'

In 1894 in a letter to Baxter Stevenson asks, 'If I were to get printed off a very few poems which are somewhat too intimate for the public, could you get them run up in some luxurious manner so that blame fools might be induced to buy them in just a sufficient quantity to pay expenses and the thing remain still in a manner private?...I should much like to get this done as a surprise for Fanny.'

The first of this group of poems acknowledges the complex ménage at the heart of the Stevenson family unit. In many ways it is one of the most sensual of all his poems. Stevenson celebrates the sexuality of both women equally. Although 'My pair of fairies plump and dark, / The dryads in my cattle park' may not be the most flattering of comparisons, he makes no distinction between the two women. When he does, it is to emphasise their different but equally strong sexual allure.

'Buxom and free, flowing and fine,

In every limb, in every line,

Inimitably feminine . . .

And the white lace (when lace they wear)

Shows on their golden breast more fair . . .

One apes the shrew, one the coquette-'

He refers to them both as his dragon-lilies, an image that morphs into tiger lilies in *Dark Women*.

## The Daughter Teuila – Her native name – The Adorner
*Vailima 1893 R.L.S. Teuila*

Stevenson again pays tribute to Belle's sexuality. In a surprising echo of twenty first century patois Stevenson calls Belle both Babe and Goddess. For Hunter Davis the poem was another piece of evidence supporting his view that she was much more than his secretary.

The poem ends with a declaration of role ambiguity last applied to Mrs Sitwell, 'Matron and child, my friend and scribe!'

## These Rings, O My Beloved Pair *Sidney March 1893 R.L.S. Teuila*

Stevenson had gone to Sidney to recuperate. Belle wrote 'he has had three topaz rings made, for topaz is the stone of his birth month, November. Inside two of them are his initials, and these he has presented, with a memorial poem, to my mother and myself. On his own we engraved the first letters of our names.

Roger C Lewis refers to an early draft which contains the significant, but ultimately rejected line, 'When from sleep my lovers arise'.

**About My Fields, in the Broad Sun** *Vailima 1892-3 B.B.S. 11*
In a letter to Ida Taylor dated 7th October 1892 Stevenson wrote; 'Nor is
Fanny any less active. Ill or well, rain or shine, a little blue indefatigable
figure is to be observed howking about certain patches of garden. She
comes in heated and bemired up to the eyebrows, late for every meal. She
has reached a sort of tragic placidity. Whenever she plants anything new,
the boys weed it up. Whenever she tries to keep anything for seed, the
house boys throw it away. And she has reached that pitch of a kind of
noble dejection that she would almost say, she did not mind.'

**Let Beauty Awake** *Songs of Travel*
The almost clichéd list of nature's charms ill prepare us for the
sensuality of the concluding two lines

**Madrigal** *Thistle Edition 1901*
For some reason *Madrigal* was omitted from *Songs of Travel* despite
featuring in the proofs. It must have been a simple error as it would
flatter any collection. 'I struck my flag at sight' would suggest that
when he vaulted through the French windows of Siron's inn it was
indeed love at first sight.

**Dark Women** *Verses 2 and 3 Songs of Travel. Variants of the poem were
published in R.L.S. Teuila, Gosse and Hellman.*
The complex publishing history of this, Stevenson's greatest love
poem, reflects layers of ambiguity and dubiety. Colvin, horrified by
the explicit references to 'the snowdrift of the bed' could only bring
himself to publish two verses in *Songs of Travel*. Belle was herself in
possession of one of the manuscript versions of the poem which was
published without stanzas 4, 5 and 9. Perhaps she chose to excise the
stanzas that were most obviously about her mother and not herself.
One of the manuscripts seen by Roger C Lewis refers to Tiger Lilies,

in the plural. Belle may have chosen to veer on the side of discretion by omitting the ambiguous reference.

The version published here is essentially Lewis' 'conflation' with the 'Take, O tiger lilies' stanza reinstated as a powerful refrain to conclude the poem. Although effective this too is only a clumsy construct given the degree of repetition with earlier lines.

### My Wife *Songs of Travel*

'Dusky,' a favourite word when describing Fanny, features again in this a simple poem of love, celebration and thanks. Janet Smith quotes from a letter that the ever pompous Colvin wrote to Gosse; 'You made no remark on the one to his wife "Dusky, trusty etc." which I wanted for its strong personal note, but which I feared might strike you as ill-written and even a little ridiculous in its first line.'

### I Know Not How it is With You *Songs of Travel*

Stevenson kept a small Buddha figure on the mantelpiece of his study (Plate 16), and there is a Buddhist like acceptance in the poem of all that has happened. Not one pebble, again a zen image, is to be changed.

### I Will Make You Brooches and Toys for Your Delight *Pall Mall Gazette 3 January 1895*

The version published here reinstates the concluding two lines of each stanza as initially published by the Boston Bibliophile Society.

Judging by the extravagant dimensions of Vailima, and the associated debt, Stevenson certainly succeeded in making a palace 'fit for you and me.' The idea that they are both tuned in to a music no one else can hear is an accurate image for whatever it was that kept the unlikely couple together.

### We Have Loved of Yore *Songs of Travel*

Stevenson returns to the persistent image of the young lovers floating dreamily among the lilies on the Loing. It was a defining and transcendent moment that assumed symbolic importance, perhaps because the emotional and sexual intensity of those endless few hours were never to be repeated. In the second half of the poem the past jostles with a future in which the Derby and Joan couple stare contentedly into the fire watching the flames shape a host of memories. In retrospect the irony is only too apparent. Stevenson may have maintained the only open fire in the whole of Samoa, but he was not destined to grow old in front of it.

Roger C Lewis identifies an earlier draft that suggests a quite different mood. After the berries and reeds the mood alters:

'Too late your love is murdered,

Too late you see before you, the love that might have been . . .

Too late the fault repented, too late the evil seen'

What was in his mind at the time? Was he feeling bitter towards Fanny, or was he harping back to another love altogether? Whatever the genesis, the final version stands as a loving tribute to his wife and an acknowledgement of the emotional continuity that bound them.


**The Stormy Evening Closes Now in Vain** *Songs of Travel*

There is a pleasing symmetry to this poem when it is placed alongside the much earlier *I sit up here at midnight,* the anguished tale of the 'foolish fisher woman' waiting for her love to return from the seas. Well now he has come home, and all is well. He attempted something similar in a letter written in Samoa and dedicated to the present generation of students drinking in Rutherford's Bar in Edinburgh. The young Stevenson who had drank and fretted about his future in the same hostelry, was at pains to reassure them that all their worries will come to nothing. (Plate 4) Similarly with this poem he is talking, reassuringly, to an earlier version of himself.

Stevenson set the poem to music, published in the Tusitala edition of his poems. In her preface Mrs Stevenson comments, 'It is said that when Mr. Kipling is heard humming a tune he is supposed to be composing a poem to fit the music. I think my husband must have used something of the same method, for in his library I found, among others, these verses written out to airs that had pleased him.'

**Verse For Her Birthday (1894)** *Vailima 10th March 1894 Memories*
The birthday poem of 1894 provides its own backcloth. Claire Harman comments that Fanny saw the war in Samoa as an extension of their marital hostilities. Stevenson may have been of the same mind. He thinks it appropriate that Fanny celebrate her fifth- fourth birthday beneath the menacing sky, to the beat of the drums of war. Certainly the turmoil to which he refers is ambiguous. However, Belle Strong wrote in her journal on the same day, 'Today is my mother's birthday, and she says the best of her presents is the piece of paper she found pinned on her mosquito-netting in the morning. It was signed RLS and addressed "To The Stormy Petrel." '

**To Belle Strong: Birthday Verses** *Vailima 18th September 1894 R.L.S. Teuila*
According to Booth and Mehew manuscript records reveal that thirty people attended an impromptu dance in Belle's honour to mark her 36th birthday. Stevenson would have enjoyed celebrating with his 'goddess bright'.

**To My Wife** *Vailima May 1894 Weir of Hermiston*
Stevenson was obviously in the habit of stealing into Fanny's room and pinning things to her curtains as this dedication to *The Weir of Hermiston* received the same treatment. They may have been the last words he wrote to his wife. It is a deeply loving testimony to the woman who

'Burnished the sword, blew on the drousy coal'. Who knows, there may be a delightful knowing reference in the last line; perhaps 'if any fire / Burn in the imperfect page, the praise be thine!' may be an oblique allusion to Fanny's earlier penchant for provoking her husband until he hurled his manuscripts into the flames. A habit that with the passage of time assumed the status of a private domestic joke. The poem is also a poignant reminder that during his last years Stevenson was haunted by the windswept hills of home. Little wonder that Fanny pursued Colvin to ensure the verse was eventually published as Stevenson had intended.

### Fixed is thy Doom *B.B.S. 11*

Although of uncertain date the final two poems both belong, thematically at least, to Stevenson's final years or months on earth. *Fixed is thy Doom*, with its Old Testament resonance is complex. The strange central image of two great eagles circling, wheeling and conferring with screams serves to emphasise the paradox of all lovers' ultimate separateness. We all die alone. With disarming honesty, Stevenson refers to the brave deception that cherishes us; the saving lie that makes life palatable, the ultimately vain hope that inspires the seaman to return from the deep, and the soldier from the ravages of war.

### Since Thou Has Given Me This Good Hope, O God *B.B.S. 11*

Here the take on death and separation is more conventional, and as such is a more appropriate poem with which to close this anthology. The verse has a grandeur and gravitas that distinguishes it from earlier attempts at the same idea. Because he has loved, because he has not lacked the loving touch of hands, he can face the azure steadfastness of death with serenity and equanimity. When all is said and done, he is the one '. . . that has a perfect friend

Her heart shall taste my laughter and my tears
And her eyes shall lead me to my end.'

# A Select Bibliography

Balfour, Graham, *The life of Robert Louis Stevenson* (London and New York), 1901, 2 vols

Bell, Ian, *Robert Louis Stevenson: Dreams of Exile* (Edinburgh), 1992

Cairney, John, *The Quest for Robert Louis Stevenson* (Edinburgh), 2004

Calder, Jenni, *RLS: A Life Study* (London),1980

Callow, Philip, *Louis: A Life of Robert Louis Stevenson* (London), 2001

Sir Sidney Colvin, Sir Sidney, *Memories and Notes* (London), 1921

Davies, Hunter, *The Teller of Tales: In Search of Robert Louis Stevenson* (London), 1994

Elwin, Malcolm, *The Strange Case of Robert Louis Stevenson* (London), 1950

Field, Field, *This Life I've Loved* (New York and Toronto), 1937

Furnas, J.C., *Voyage to Windward: The life of Robert Louis Stevenson* (London), 1952

Hamilton, Clayton, *On the trail of Stevenson* (London and New York), 1923

Harman, Claire, *Robert Louis Stevenson: A Biography* (London), 2005

Hellman, George, *The True Stevenson: A Study in Clarification* (Boston), 1925

Hennessy, James Pope, *Robert Louis Stevenson* (London), 1974

Johnstone, Arthur, *Recollections of Robert Louis Stevenson in the Pacific* (London), 1905

Knight, Alanna, *RLS in The South Seas* (Edinburgh), 1986

Koestenbaum, Wayne, *Double Talk: The Erotics of Male Literary Collaboration* (New York and London), 1989

Lapierre, Alexandra, *Fanny Stevenson: Muse, Adventuress and Romantic Enigma* (London), 1995

Lucas, E.V., *The Colvins and Their Friends* (London), 1928

MacKay, Margaret, *The Violent Friend: The Story of Mrs Robert Louis Stevenson* 1840–1914 (London), 1969

McLynn, Frank, *Robert Louis Stevenson: A Biography* (London), 1993

Masson, Rosiline, (ed.), *I Can Remember Robert Louis Stevenson* (Edinburgh), 1925

Masson, Rosiline, *Life of Robert Louis Stevenson* (Edinburgh and London), 1923

Moors, H.J., *With Stevenson in Samoa* (London), 1911

Osbourne, Katherine D., *Robert Louis Stevenson in California* (Chicago), 1911

Steuart, John A., *The Cap of Youth* (Philadelphia and London), 1927

Sanchez, Nellie Vandegrift, *The Life of Mrs Robert Louis Stevenson* (New York), 1920

Stevenson, Fanny and Robert, *Our Samoan Adventure*, ed. Charles Neider (London), 1956

# Index of First Lines